WITHDRAWN
FROM STOCK
MUL LIBRARY

QM Library

23 1267746 0

PN1998.A3.P4 WAR

MAIN LIBRARY
QUEEN MARY, UNIVERSITY OF LONDON

D1615685

Maurice Pialat

MANCHESTER
1824

Manchester University Press

FRENCH FILM DIRECTORS

DIANA HOLMES and ROBERT INGRAM *series editors*
DUDLEY ANDREW *series consultant*

Jean-Jacques Beineix   PHIL POWRIE

Luc Besson   SUSAN HAYWARD

Bertrand Blier   SUE HARRIS

Robert Bresson   KEITH READER

Leos Carax   GARIN DOWD AND FERGUS DALEY

Claude Chabrol   GUY AUSTIN

Jean Cocteau   JAMES WILLIAMS

Claire Denis   MARTINE BEUGNET

Marguerite Duras   RENATE GÜNTHER

Georges Franju   KATE INCE

Jean-Luc Godard   DOUGLAS MORREY

Diane Kurys   CARRIE TARR

Patrice Leconte   LISA DOWNING

Louis Malle   HUGO FREY

Georges Méliès   ELIZABETH EZRA

Jean Renoir   MARTIN O'SHAUGHNESSY

Alain Resnais   EMMA WILSON

Coline Serreau   BRIGITTE ROLLET

François Truffaut   DIANA HOLMES AND ROBERT INGRAM

Agnès Varda   ALISON SMITH

Jean Vigo   MICHAEL TEMPLE

FRENCH FILM DIRECTORS

Maurice Pialat

MARJA WAREHIME

Manchester University Press
MANCHESTER AND NEW YORK

distributed exclusively in the USA by Palgrave

Copyright © Marja Warehime 2006

The right of Marja Warehime to be identified as the author of this work has
been asserted by her in accordance with the Copyright, Designs and Patents
Act 1988.

Published by Manchester University Press
Oxford Road, Manchester M13 9NR, UK
and Room 400, 175 Fifth Avenue, New York, NY 10010, USA
www.manchesteruniversitypress.co.uk

Distributed exclusively in the USA by
Palgrave, 175 Fifth Avenue, New York, NY 10010, USA

Distributed exclusively in Canada by
UBC Press, University of British Columbia, 2029 West Mall, Vancouver,
BC, Canada v6T 1z2

British Library Cataloguing-in-Publication Data
A catalogue record for this book is available from the British Library

Library of Congress Cataloging-in-Publication Data applied for

ISBN 0 7190 6822 3 *hardback*
EAN 978 0 7190 6822 5

First published 2006

15 14 13 12 11 10 09 08 07 06   10 9 8 7 6 5 4 3 2 1

QM LIBRARY
(MILE END)

Typeset in Scala with Meta display
by Koinonia, Manchester
Printed in Great Britain
by Bell & Bain Ltd, Glasgow

Contents

List of plates

Every effort has been made to contact the holders of the rights to these photographs. If any proper acknowledgement has not been made, please contact Manchester University Press.

Series editors' foreword

To an anglophone audience, the combination of the words 'French' and 'cinema' evokes a particular kind of film: elegant and wordy, sexy but serious – an image as dependent on national stereotypes as is that of the crudely commercial Hollywood blockbuster, which is not to say that either image is without foundation. Over the past two decades, this generalised sense of a significant relationship between French identity and film has been explored in scholarly books and articles, and has entered the curriculum at university level and, in Britain, at A-level. The study of film as an art-form and (to a lesser extent) as industry, has become a popular and widespread element of French Studies, and French cinema has acquired an important place within Film Studies. Meanwhile, the growth in multi-screen and 'art-house' cinemas, together with the development of the video industry, has led to the greater availability of foreign-language films to an English-speaking audience. Responding to these developments, this series is designed for students and teachers seeking information and accessible but rigorous critical study of French cinema, and for the enthusiastic filmgoer who wants to know more.

The adoption of a director-based approach raises questions about *auteurism*. A series that categorises films not according to period or to genre (for example), but to the person who directed them, runs the risk of espousing a romantic view of film as the product of solitary inspiration. On this model, the critic's role might seem to be that of discovering continuities, revealing a necessarily coherent set of themes and motifs which correspond to the particular genius of the individual. This is not our aim: the *auteur* perspective on film, itself most clearly articulated in France in the early 1950s, will be interrogated in certain volumes of the series, and, throughout, the director will be treated as one highly significant element in a complex process of film production and reception which includes socio-economic and political determinants, the work of a large and highly skilled team of artists and technicians, the mechanisms of production and distribution, and the complex and multiply determined responses of spectators.

The work of some of the directors in the series is already known outside France, that of others is less so – the aim is both to provide informative and original English-language studies of established figures, and to extend the range of French directors known to anglophone students of cinema. We intend the series to contribute to the promotion of the informal and formal study of French films, and to the pleasure of those who watch them.

DIANA HOLMES
ROBERT INGRAM

Acknowledgements

It would be inaccurate, but not entirely wrong, to say that this book was inspired by Sandrine Bonnaire's missing dimple in *A nos amours*. The brief moment when Maurice Pialat, as 'Suzanne's' father, teases her about having only one dimple left has always seemed, to the naive viewer I still remain, heart-stoppingly real.

I would like to thank Gaumont for its gracious permission to use five of the photographs that figure in this book. My thanks also to Monique Prim for the authorisation to use work by her late husband Bernard Prim. I very much appreciated the advice of Catherine Frochen at the Photothèque at *Cahiers du cinéma* and am very grateful to the staff of the Bibliothèque du film for providing photographs from its collections.

I also want to express my appreciation to the staffs of the Bibliothèque Nationale and the Institut National de l'Audiovisuel (INA), and in particular to Laurent Bismuth for his welcome to the collections at the INA. The staff at the INA made it possible for me to view a copy of *Passe ton bac d'abord* and I could not have completed this book without their help. I owe equal thanks to the staff of the Thomas Cooper Library's Interlibrary Loan Department at the University of South Carolina for locating what is apparently the only video copy of *La Gueule ouverte* in North America. I am extremely grateful to the University of Iowa for responding to their appeal and being willing to lend it to me.

Some of the material on *Van Gogh* in Chapter 6 was published in a slightly different form in the journal *Sites* 6:2 (2002), pp. 56–67. I thank the journal for permission to reproduce this material and refer readers to its website (*www.tandf.co.uk/journals*).

My thanks also to my graduate assistant Jonathon Allen for help in typing Pialat's filmography. Finally, I would like to thank my husband for his support and encouragement, and for appreciating my creative use of commas. I dedicate this book to him – and also to the memory of my father.

Introduction: Maurice Pialat, the outsider

To call Maurice Pialat a 'marginal du centre' (literally a 'central marginal figure', a pivotal or influential outsider) – as *Cahiers du cinéma* did in 1983 – suggests the contradictions of Pialat's career and sums up the difficulties of categorising the work of one of the most important and idiosyncratic figures of the post New Wave (Bergala 1983: 20). Pialat's work inspires comparison with such legendary figures as Jean Renoir and Robert Bresson, yet he does not have the international reputation one might expect, given his gifts as a director and his importance in French cinema history. Pialat's death in 2003 inevitably situated him as a filmmaker of the 1980s, the decade in which his work began to receive serious critical attention and attract a broader public. Yet by 1983, when *A nos amours* won the prestigious Prix Louis Delluc and the César for best film, he had been making films for over twenty years.

That is not to say that his work has lacked either critical acclaim or official recognition. His first *court métrage*, the documentary *L'Amour existe*, won both the Prix Louis Lumière in 1961 and an award at the Venice Film Festival; his first full-length film, *L'Enfance nue,* won the Prix Jean Vigo in 1969. In 1972, Jean Yanne received the César for best actor in Pialat's first commercial success, *Nous ne vieillirons pas ensemble.* After *A nos amours* came out in 1983, the newspaper *Libération* proclaimed 'Pialat est grand' (Pialat is great). In 1987 Pialat was awarded La Palme d'or (Golden Palm), the ultimate recognition given at Cannes, for his adaptation of Georges Bernanos's novel *Sous le soleil de Satan*, starring Sandrine Bonnaire and Gérard Depardieu. His last major film, *Van Gogh*, was one of only two French entries in competition for the Palme d'or in May of 1991. The film was also nominated in twelve other categories and brought Jacques Dutronc the César for best actor. Joël Magny, who wrote the first (and for many years, only) important book-length appraisal of Pialat's work in French, judged *Van Gogh* to be 'incontestablement une des œuvres majeures du cinéma français des vingt dernières années'[1] (Magny 1992: 9).

Nonetheless, Pialat never became a popular director like Renoir or François Truffaut and – despite being of Truffaut's generation – he was unable to launch his career during the vogue for young directors that followed the early successes of the New Wave. Truffaut came to his rescue and financed the completion of *L'Enfance nue* in 1968, but Pialat's difficulties in obtaining adequate financing ultimately limited his ability to make films. His output, for a major director, is far closer to that of Robert Bresson than Truffaut or the even more prolific Chabrol. Pialat's reputation rests primarily on ten full-length films (although this does not include *La Maison des bois*, 'The House in the woods,' a seven-part television series, unavailable at the time this was written).

Ironically, however, in 1998 when *Cahiers du cinéma* invited a number of young, gifted, and influential directors (Olivier Assayas, Claire Denis, Cédric Kahn and Noémie Lvovsky) to consider the importance of the *Nouvelle Vague* in the development of their work, the conversation veered off into a discussion of Maurice Pialat. Cédric Kahn insisted that 'Ce sont les films de Pialat qui m'ont surtout impressionné. Je ne dois pas être le seul car il exerce une énorme influence sur tous les jeunes cinéastes ... Pourquoi ne fait-il pas parti de la *Nouvelle Vague*, s'en est il toujours senti exclu?'[2] (Assayas *et al.* 1998: 72). Filmmaker Arnaud Desplechin said much the same thing in an earlier interview with Antoine de Baecque and Thierry Jousse of *Cahiers*: 'le cinéaste qui a l'influence la plus forte et la plus constante

1 'Indisputably one of the major works of French cinema in the last twenty years'. (All translations from French are my own unless otherwise indicated.)

2 'Pialat's films are the ones that have particularly impressed me. I must not be the only one because he has an enormous influence on young filmmakers ... Why isn't he considered part of the New Wave, why did he always feel he was excluded from it?' (I have translated the label '*Nouvelle Vague*' here, but will use the terms 'New Wave' and '*Nouvelle Vague*' synonymously throughout this volume.)

sur le jeune cinéma français, ce n'est pas Jean-Luc Godard mais Maurice Pialat'[3] (De Baecque *et al.* 1996: 100).

Noémie Lvovsky inadvertently suggested one reason why Pialat never achieved the recognition given to New Wave directors when she remarked on the playfulness of New Wave films. The light-hearted moments in Truffaut's films made her love the experience of seeing movies, going to the theatre, waiting for the lights to go down; seeing the images flickering on the screen. By contrast, Pialat's films had such an emotional impact that they were intimidating: 'je n'ai jamais autant eu l'impression de voir du désespoir, de l'amour ou de la haine, comme en bloc. Comme si [Pialat] pouvait vraiment toucher les sentiments que l'on peut connaître dans la vie'[4] (Assayas *et al.* 1998: 72). The wrenching emotional power of Pialat's work, its intelligence, the seriousness of its moral universe and its uncompromising rejection of conventional aesthetic and dramatic effects are difficult to reconcile with the notion of film as entertainment. In fact, it is one of the profound contradictions of Pialat's career that he desired to be a truly popular filmmaker, but did not try to please. He made few concessions to popular tastes, deliberately treating difficult, even repellent subjects without glossing over their less attractive aspects, while his often highly fragmented narratives demanded a good deal of his viewer. In fact, despite his antipathy toward the academy, he was in many ways a filmmaker's filmmaker, at times agonising over the smallest formal details of his work – even though, as an interviewer once reminded him, most people only saw a film once and would not notice them (Pialat 1992: 106). However, Pialat's status as an outsider in French film history has almost as much to do with the filmmaker's reputation as man and a director as with his films. As he himself pointed out, 'quand on fait des œuvres violentes, dérangeantes, comment être sage comme une image?'[5] (Pialat 1980: 9).

Pialat changed his image by growing a beard in the 1980s, but a photograph of him taken during the filming of *Nous ne vieillirons pas ensemble* in 1972 shows a clean-shaven man with strong features

3 'The director who has the strongest and most consistent influence on young French filmmakers is not Jean-Luc Godard, but Maurice Pialat'.

4 'I have never had such a strong impression of seeing outright despair, love or hate. As though [Pialat] could actually touch emotions that you feel in real life'.

5 'When you make violent, disturbing films how can you be nice and well-behaved?'.

beneath a rebellious shock of dark hair, which fell like a fringe over his forehead. He faces the camera but looks away from it, half-scowling, his arms folded across his chest in a gesture both defiant and self-protective. Compactly built, stocky, he fits Gérard Depardieu's description: 'ce fils d'Auvergnat au cou de taureau et aux mains de forgeron ... un vrai taureau de combat'[6] (Depardieu 1988: 75, 94). However, Pialat's interviews reveal an extremely vulnerable artist, self-critical and endlessly denigrating his work, impossible to reassure, uncertain about his talent and his achievements, but also angry and resentful that his work did not receive greater recognition.

If the name Pialat is not without significance to the French film-going public, it is partly because he acquired the reputation of a singularly difficult and demanding director, or to put it more bluntly, an *emmerdeur* (pain in the arse) who provoked and psychologically abused his actors and collaborators (De Baecque 1992: 51). 'Tu avais l'art de toucher là où ça fait mal, d'inciser les névroses à vif, d'éclairer d'une lumière crue les faiblesses les plus soigneusement cachées. Chapeau!', Gérard Depardieu wrote him some years after the filming of *Loulou*[7] (Depardieu 1988: 7). However, during the filming he was furious with Pialat, declaring openly in an interview that 'c'est de la merde ce qu'on fait. Quand je pense que les gens vont payer dix-huit mille balles pour voir ça!'[8] (Gonzales 1985: 144). Depardieu was by no means the only one to complain, as Pialat frequently clashed with his leading male actors, or at least more frequently than his female leads. Although in the case of Sophie Marceau, the press reported that Pialat tortured her during the filming of *Police*, and she also adamantly declared that she would never work with him again (De Baecque 1992: 51).

Relationships with his writers and crew were also problematic: Pialat regularly complained about technicians in interviews, and sometimes went through a series of directors of photography and/or film editors on a single film. Four directors of photography were credited for *A nos amours*, along with seven film editors, and there

6 'A son of Auvergne with a bull's neck and blacksmith's hands ... a real fighting bull'.
7 'You had the gift for finding the tender spots, for cutting to the quick of neuroses, for shining a bright light on the most carefully hidden weaknesses. Well done!'
8 'What we're doing is shit. When I think people will pay real money to see this!'.

were several directors of photography for *Van Gogh* (De Baecque 1992: 51). Pialat's creative relationship with Arlette Langmann proved both productive and durable, but he 'courted' Catherine Breillat's collaboration during the making of *Loulou* only to 'break up' with her (their differences were settled in court) during the filming of *Police*. However, Pialat's reputation as an *emmerdeur* did not keep major actors and actresses from working with him. Sandrine Bonnaire, whom Pialat discovered while casting *A nos amours*, remained attached to him, claiming he was more like a member of her family than a director (Bonnaire 2003: 41). Perhaps the most balanced and revealing appraisal comes from Evelyne Ker, whose difficulties in playing the unflattering role of Bonnaire's mother in *A nos amours* give her remarks particular credence.

> On le présente comme un sadique, un bourreau. On m'avait dit: 'tu vas vivre un enfer'. En fait, il ne faut pas exagérer. Car sur le tournage on s'amusait souvent beaucoup. Il y avait une grosse complicité et de grosses rigolades. Maurice Pialat, c'est vrai, a aussi besoin de psychodrame, de tension pour créer. Alors il y avait des affrontements. Selon ses angoisses, selon ses jours, il a sa tête de turc. Il faut qu'il se passe 'quelque chose' qui vienne des autres pour que le déclic chez lui fonctionne, sinon il s'ennuie, il tourne à vide. Mais quand c'est parti, c'est sans limite, c'est un moment de vie donné, il nous bouffe![9] (Pialat 1984: 152)

If Pialat's reputation was partly a media creation and a convenient shelter for a complicated artist, his hostility to the film community contributed to his marginalisation, although clearly it did not keep him from commercial or critical success. In fact, as Antoine de Baecque points out, with four films (*A nos amours, Police, Sous le soleil de Satan* and *Van Gogh*), Pialat attracted over four million viewers – more viewers than all of the directors of the *Nouvelle Vague* put together (De Baecque 1992: 56).

9 'People see him as a sadist, a torturer. They told me "you are going to go through hell". In fact, we shouldn't exaggerate. Because during the shooting we often had a good time. There was a tremendous bond between us and lots of jokes. Maurice Pialat, it's true, also needs psychodrama, tension, in order to create. So there were conflicts. Depending on his anxieties, depending on the day, he has his scapegoats. Something had to come from us that got him started, if not he was bored; he got nothing done. But when we got started, it was endless, like life itself, he just ate us up!'

The scandal of Cannes 1987

Perhaps one of the most telling moments in Maurice Pialat's on-going relationship with film and the French film-going public was the 'scandal' at Cannes over the attribution of the Palme d'or in 1987. Viewers watching television coverage of the 40th Festival on Antenne 2 would have seen Yves Montand, who was the head of the jury that year, standing centre stage, looking tired but elegant in a black tuxedo with a red carnation *boutonnière*. When Montand pronounced 'la Palme d'or à l'unanimité à Maurice Pialat' ('The Golden Palm unanimously goes to Maurice Pialat') there was applause, but mingled with shouts and whistles. As Pialat rose and made his way to the stage, a man in the audience, apparently too near a microphone, could clearly be heard by the television audience over the noise exclaiming 'Ah ce salaud!' ('Ah that bastard!') and then in a more resigned ironic tone, 'c'est Cannes' ('that's Cannes for you').

Pialat could not have heard this, although he could hardly have been unaware that the audience was not unanimously delighted with the announcement. Yet he was smiling as he moved towards the stage. Dressed very simply in a light beige cardigan over a white shirt and wearing a black bowtie, it was as though he had never expected to be in the spotlight. After he accepted the award, he turned to the audience and said in a low, even tone, with perfect composure: 'Aujourd'hui vous me donnez l'occasion de parler, je serai très bref. Je vous réponds. Je ne devais pas faillir à ma réputation, je suis surtout content ce soir pour tous les cris et les sifflets que vous m'adressez, et si vous ne m'aimez pas je peux vous dire que je ne vous aime pas non plus'.[10] He then raised his right arm and jabbed his fist in the air in a gesture of victory. Given his reputation, it was probably only to be expected that a number of commentators erroneously reported this as an indecent gesture, but the scandal gave ever greater currency to the perception of Maurice Pialat as vulgar and rude, lacking both grace and graciousness. However, it is a prime example of his willingness, even eagerness, to transform his very real success into a rejection that confirmed his position as an outsider.

10 'Today you give me the occasion to speak, and I shall be very brief. Here is my response. I should not fail to uphold my reputation. I am particularly pleased by all the protests and whistles directed at me this evening, and if you do not like me, I can say that I do not like you either.'

Pialat may have deliberately cultivated his status as an outsider, unable to see himself as anything other than 'not one of them', but the label also accurately reflects the fact that he never sought to associate himself with any group or movement, despite lamenting his solitude as a filmmaker. Nonetheless, in the mid-1970s he was briefly lumped in with a 'tendency' dubbed the *Le Nouveau Naturel* or 'New Naturalism' by *Télérama*, whose critics lauded a constellation of films by younger filmmakers that seemed to herald a fresh approach. Primarily associated with directors such as Pascal Thomas (*Les Zozos*, 1972, *Pleure pas la bouche pleine*, 1973); Gérard Guérin (*Lo Païs*, 1972); Joël Séria (*Charlie et ses deux nénettes*, 1973); Philippe Condroyer (*La Coupe à dix francs*, 1974), the critics at *Télérama* also linked this new tendency to the work of Pialat, Jacques Rozier, Jacques Doillon and Jean Eustache.

Télérama critics saw *Le Nouveau Naturel* as a cinema that adopted the programme of the *Nouvelle Vague* – small budgets, reduced film crews, location filming, personal stories rather than literary adaptations – but turned its back on Paris to focus on the lives and problems of ordinary people in the provinces: a cabinet maker, a poster hanger, provincial schoolboys, a baker's assistant, secretaries looking for work. *Télérama* praised the apparent spontaneity and improvisational feel of these films as well as the fact that they opened a window into the lives of ordinary people and starred relatively new, young talents. (Trémois 1974: 65). Ultimately, however, Pialat proved to have much more in common with Rozier, Eustache and Doillon in his commitment to auteur cinema. In the case of Rozier and Eustache in particular he also shared an uncompromising approach to filmmaking that discouraged producers from taking on his projects.

Neither a member of a group nor a mentor, as was Truffaut, to a host of aspiring filmmakers, Pialat nonetheless touched a younger generation, as the *Cahiers* roundtable made clear. Moreover, his early films in particular prefigure the 'neo-realism' of the nineties, films (by Dominique Cabréra, Bruno Dumont, Tony Gatlif, Robert Guédiguian, Manuel Poirier, Sandrine Veysset, Eric Zonca, among others) critical of French society, films made on small or limited budgets that focus on ordinary people (many played by non-professional actors) who are socially, culturally, geographically or economically marginalised (Beugnet 2003: 351). However, to the degree that Pialat explored his own private universe through his films, gradually developing a very personal approach to filmmaking, he more closely resembles Robert Bresson, despite the profound differences that separate them. Both were trained as painters before becoming filmmakers, both were demanding artists whose uncompromising way of working (and difficulties with financing their work) prevented them from producing a large body of films. Curiously, despite their differences in approach, both decided to adapt the work of novelist Georges Bernanos for the screen. However, the crucial link between them is an obsession with a particular kind of cinematic truth – each representing a different kind of absolute, a *cas limite* that discourages followers or cinematic 'offspring'.

Pialat and Bresson

Superficially, nothing could seem further from the 'naturalism' (although Pialat rejected the label) of Pialat's work, where eros, love, hate and death have an overwhelming material reality, than the 'spiritual style' of Bresson's films. Many of the adjectives most frequently applied to Bresson's work: austerity, rigour, formal perfection, seem totally foreign to that of Pialat, who consistently denounced the *carences* (deficiencies) of his work and frequently accused himself of laziness and lack of preparation (Pialat 1983: 7). Susan Sontag considered Bresson a master of the reflective mode where 'the pull toward emotional detachment is counterbalanced by elements in the work that promote distance, disinterestedness, impartiality' (Sontag 1967: 177). For Bresson, the emotional intensity of art was inseparable from a certain detachment, even 'coldness'. In fact, when Bresson recalled his reaction to reading the narrative of the prison escape that he would adapt to make *Un condamné à mort s'est échappé*, he noted that 'il y avait à la fois cette froideur et cette simplicité qui font que l'on sent que c'est l'œuvre d'un homme qui écrit avec son cœur'[11] (Bresson 1957: 4).

By contrast, Pialat can only be considered a 'hot-tempered' artist and the expression of powerful emotion – *à chaud* – represents such a crucial element of Pialat's cinematic universe that he deliberately sacrificed the formal quality of the filmic images in order to obtain it.

11 'there was both that coldness and that simplicity that make one feel that it is the work of a man who writes with his heart'.

Critics reproached him for including shots that were less than perfect, technically or otherwise, where the image was slightly out of focus, under or overexposed; where a microphone was visible in the frame. In his last film, *Le Garçu*, reflections of the film crew appear in the window of a bus. Yet Pialat inevitably weighed the authenticity of the emotions expressed in these images against their formal imperfections.

Bresson also remains a world apart from Pialat in avoiding violent or powerfully dramatic events. For Pialat, making a film involved provoking, and capturing extreme moments and conflicting emotions; he forced viewers to confront situations that in some cases they found offensive, or at the very least uncomfortable. He does not spare the viewer the physical degradation of the dying mother in *La Gueule ouverte*, or the physical brutality of Jean's jealous rages in *Nous ne vieillirons pas ensemble*; the father's outrageous intrusion to settle old scores during a family celebration in *A nos amours*, or the last desperate effort of the rejected child in *L'Enfance nue* who, the very morning the social worker is coming to take him away, spends all of the money his foster father had guiltily slipped under his pillow the night before to buy his foster mother an expensive silk scarf.

Yet Pialat, like Bresson, rejected the conventional psychological drama of the 1950s where the filmmaker develops a character or series of characters, then relies on the spectator's understanding of the characters' psychology to create tension or suspense and build scenes to a dramatic crescendo. Pialat never links scenes to construct a character, set up a dramatic moment or underline a humorous or ironic one. Like Bresson, Pialat tends to displace the burden of psychology onto form (Reader 1998: 3), yet generally eschews special effects, if not occasional extraordinary camera movements. Pialat even lamented his (relatively infrequent) use of music, as though this represented an admission of formal weakness or a lapse in taste.

His narratives, like Bresson's, are often highly fragmented; his use of ellipsis as bold and striking as any in Bresson's films. However, where Bresson tends to cut out the violent centre of the dramatic action, Pialat dispenses with scenes which lead up to or follow dramatic moments. He consistently eliminates scenes whose function would be – if they existed – purely explicative or anecdotal: 'On fait une scène et puis on passe à autre chose; pas de graisse',[12] Pialat

12 'You do a scene and then you go on to something else; no fat.'

maintained in an interview in the late seventies (Pialat 1979b: 16). In both cases the narrative fragmentation leaves the connection between sequences ambiguous, making it practically impossible to determine the duration of the filmic events.

Central to both Bresson and Pialat's creative work is their relationship with the men and women who figure in their films. For Pialat 'le moment où les acteurs sont devant la caméra représente au moins 80% du film ... tout le reste c'est du bataclan'[13] (Pialat 2000: 63). Bresson's approach to his actors reflected his considerable distaste for conventional films where – in his view – professional 'actors' merely playacted. Ultimately he worked exclusively with amateurs he called *modèles* chosen for their physical and moral resemblance to the characters they were to incarnate. He then extracted the essence of this resemblance by forcing them through the endless rehearsals and many takes required to school them in the emotional inexpressiveness, automatic gestures and the particular flat, neutral tone he desired. While Jean-Pierre Oudart noted the Sadean rapport between Bresson and his 'models', Bresson, unlike Pialat, never acquired the reputation of abusing his actors (Oudart 1972: 88). And yet Pialat's way of working, for all its *sturm und drang*, represented a far greater degree of generosity and trust precisely because it offered actors a form of creative collaboration neither possible nor desirable within the Bressonian system.

Pialat also frequently worked with amateurs who sometimes played themselves, using their own names as the names of their characters. He much admired the work of the father in *Passe ton bac d'abord*, who was in fact the father of one of the younger principals of the film, precisely because, as he put it, 'il parvient à exprimer ce que les meilleurs acteurs parviennent parfois à faire: sa vérité, et ce qu'il joue là, est exactement à la hauteur de ce qu'il est'[14] (Pialat 1979b: 13). However, Pialat did not share Bresson's disdain for professional actors, drawing powerful performances from them and sometimes using them against type: Depardieu, large and stocky, took on the role of Bernanos's ascetic and self-flagellating priest; Jacques Dutronc (as emaciated as Depardieu was heavy) ironic and taciturn, gave a new

13 'the moment the actors are in front of the camera represents at least 80 per cent of the film, the rest is just details'.

14 'he manages to express what the best actors sometimes manage to express: his truth and the way he acts corresponds exactly to who he is'.

dimension to the role of the tormented Van Gogh. Pialat's casts frequently mixed professionals and non-professionals, to whom he provided minimal direction (to the point where Sophie Marceau, among others, claimed he left them adrift) precisely because he expected them to invent themselves in front of the camera rather than memorise a script.

Bresson's *modèles*' careful modulation of tone, their precise diction and the otherworldly quality of their delivery, coupled with the literariness of Bresson's dialogues, led Marguerite Duras to marvel that she had 'entendu une langue admirable dans Bresson qui est le français'[15] (Duras 1997: 49). By contrast, Pialat's characters not only use bad grammar, clichés, slang and vulgar expressions, but under the pressure of an emotionally charged situation they frequently stumble, stop, grope for words, lose their focus or let their sentences trail off. The dialogue in Pialat's films is not always intelligible, or even significant, because Pialat considered that as much if not more of the meaning of any exchange was conveyed by expression and gesture than by what was said. And, like Bresson, Pialat understood the importance of silence – sometimes stretching it out unbearably – and the importance of sound, as opposed to language.

Despite their very different approach to actors and to the act of filming, Pialat was no less obsessed with authenticity than Bresson. Yet where Bresson aimed to arrive at truth through the discipline of rehearsals, Pialat worked more instinctively, sometimes with little in the way of a script. The degree to which Pialat was willing to rely on improvisation recalls Renoir, but Pialat increasingly sought to orchestrate and capture the tense or intense moments in which the actors appeared to forget their roles and invest their own emotional capital in the ongoing action. His particular form of realism derives from his conviction that the act of filming is itself a form of lived reality – and ultimately the only reality the filmmaker can convey. His approach puts considerable stress on the director, who must maintain an unfocused yet total concentration on the actors and the unfolding scene in order to guide the action without controlling it, an effort Pialat compared to automatic writing.

Although Pialat often expressed the desire to work every day, 'comme on va à l'usine' ('like working in a factory') his production

15 'heard an admirable language in Bresson, which is French'.

was marked by discontinuity (Pialat 1983: 13). Spikes of high-voltage creative activity during the filming were followed by his withdrawal – sometimes episodically during the filming, but more frequently as it ended – occasioned by fatigue or depression. During these moments he reassessed his work and took stock of his creative progress. His legendary tendency to self-destruct during the course of making a film reflected the intensity with which he pursued his dream of an ideal cinema: 'un cinéma où il n'y aurait plus de temps, où l'on s'enfoncerait dans ce qu'on a à dire et on le dirait vraiment' [16] (Pialat 1983: 7).

Ultimately each film offered him the chance to express what he 'had to say' through a struggle with the various elements of material resistance presented by the film: the scenario, time constraints, budget restrictions, scheduling and technical problems, conflicts or difficulties with actors, all of which required him to improvise and to invent. His ability, not merely to salvage difficult situations of one kind or another, but to turn them to advantage by making them serve his expressive aims was arguably one of his greatest sources of artistic satisfaction. 'J'en ai quand même fait de belles' he reminisced in his last interview with *Cahiers du cinéma*, 'il ne doit pas y en avoir beaucoup dans l'histoire du cinéma qui engagent des acteurs qui ne peuvent pas parler et des actrices qui ne peuvent pas jouer. Or, j'ai fait les deux avec des résultats'[17] (Pialat 2000: 68).

Joël Magny suggests that Pialat's approach reflects his training as a painter because he treated his films as though they were canvases he could rework by adding a touch here or there, or even painting out entire sections in order to try something different. Inevitably, however, the 'painterly' approach requires not only great patience but the courage and the audacity to risk putting everything into question each time work resumes – even though this engages the work of an entire crew of actors and technicians and wreaks havoc with film budgets. 'Time' then becomes both the director's greatest luxury and his greatest enemy. In fact, to Pialat's great discomfiture, most of his films were not completed in a single block, but were interrupted by a

16 'a cinema where time would no longer exist, where you would go deeply into what you had to say and really say it'.

17 'I've really managed some good ones [...] There mustn't be many in the history of film who hire actors who can't speak and actresses who can't act. Well, I've done both with results'.

break of from several weeks to a year before shooting could resume. Emmanuel Schlumberger, who represented Gaumont's interests as producer and distributor for both *Loulou* and *A nos amours,* noted that 'il vaut mieux [...] ne pas compter sur [Pialat] pour livrer un film à date fixe, après exécution d'un plan de travail rigoureux[18] (Pialat 1984: 145). Yet the luxury of time takes on a more existential dimension in Pialat's career precisely because he began to work 'late,' ten years late by his own count, and because each film required such a significant investment of his own creative energy. 'Toute œuvre créatrice est une lutte contre la mort', he asserted in an interview that put his 'laziness' into a more Freudian perspective: 'ne pas faire', he claimed, 'par paresse, c'est garder toujours l'impression qu'on le pourra encore, qu'on a beaucoup de temps devant soi' [19] (Pialat 1984: 14).

A life in cinema

Pascal Mérigeau's *Pialat* represents the closest approach to an official biography of the filmmaker, although Pialat's failing health and his reservations about the project kept him from collaborating with the author. Yet Pialat made it clear that his films had an important autobiographical dimension. He saw *La Gueule ouverte* as an effort to come to terms with his mother's death, while *Nous ne vieillirons pas ensemble* was based on the novel he wrote about his love affair with Colette, a woman much his junior. Pialat also maintained that his first full-length film, *L'Enfance nue*, was totally autobiographical, despite the fact that, unlike the main character, he had never been put up for adoption (Pialat 1980: 5). In short, the main character in Pialat's films is frequently a symbolic stand-in for Pialat himself, and as Michel Boujut observed, 'tout film *de* Maurice Pialat est un film *sur* Maurice Pialat'[20] (Pialat 1984: 174). The biographical sketch that follows owes much to Mérigeau's work, as well as to the many published interviews both with Pialat and his collaborators.

18 'it is best [...] not to count on [Pialat] to deliver a film by a particular date, according to a strict work schedule'.
19 'Every creative work is a battle against death [...] not to do something out of laziness allows you to keep the impression that you could still do it, that you have a good deal of time ahead of you'.
20 'every film *by* Maurice Pialat is a film *about* Maurice Pialat'.

Maurice Pialat was born 31 August 1925 to middle-class parents in Cunlhat, Puy-de-Dôme, where his father ran a small business selling wood and coal inherited after his father's death. There is clearly a parallel between the father in *La Gueule ouverte,* whose haphazardly run 'Boutique de la laine' (Wool Boutique) has only its prime location to recommend it, and Pialat's own father, whose store lost money so rapidly he was forced to declare bankruptcy only two years after taking over the business. Pialat was just two when his parents moved to a furnished apartment in the Paris suburb of Courbevoie. His father drove a truck for Banania, a powdered breakfast drink, then sold metal blinds and awnings. There would be no other children. Though he was too young to understand the loss of status involved in the move to Courbevoie, or his parents' anxiety and dismay over their financial reverses, Pialat later connected his father's falling ill during the years after their move to his being unable to adjust to working as a truck driver.

His parents were constantly short of money, and when Maurice was four, they sent him to stay with his maternal grandparents in Villeneuve-Saint-Georges in order to make it possible for his mother to work. While his parents visited him on Sundays, Maurice apparently felt abandoned, even though he was close to his grandparents, perhaps closer than to his parents. His earliest childhood memory, of loco-motives puffing smoke as they went under the Villeneuve-Triage bridge, was linked to his maternal grandfather, who had a manage-ment position with the *Chemin de fer du Nord* (Northern Railway). Pialat was about eight years old when he first discovered films. His parents, no doubt for financial reasons, rarely went to the movies, so it was primarily on Thursday afternoons when there were no classes that he saw Chaplin shorts, Laurel and Hardy, and other films deemed suitable for his age. The neighbourhood theatres he frequented later were clearly enchanted places evoked by the litany of their names: 'Palace, Eden, Magic, Lux, Kursaal' in the voice-over narration of his 1961 documentary *L'Amour existe.* His love for the popular Saturday night cinema of his childhood and adolescence indelibly marked his approach to film. His first cinematic love affair was with Jean Renoir's 1938 film, *La Bête humaine,* which he credited with inspiring his vocation, even though he did not turn to film until after he abandoned painting – in his early twenties.

When Pialat's maternal grandmother died she left the family

enough money to invest in a small business, and the family moved to another Paris suburb, Montreuil-sous-bois, to take over a shop selling newspapers and magazines. When France fell to the Germans, Pialat's parents fled to Clermont-Ferrand, but soon returned to Montreuil. *L'Amour existe* evokes the grim years of the Occupation, although they did not lead Pialat to political engagement, either as a collaborator or a member of the Resistance (Mérigeau 2002: 25).

Pialat decided to leave school when he learned he would have to repeat a grade, lamenting later that he did not develop better writing skills (Pialat 1995: 33). His sense of lost possibilities led him to identify with the working-class adolescents he filmed in *Passe ton bac d'abord* – whose wasted education leaves them without much of a future – rather than with his own family where for several generations on either side the men were solidly bourgeois (Pialat 1980b: 31). In 1942, when he was seventeen, Pialat met Micheline, who would become his first wife; they both sang in the choir of their parish church. He worked briefly for an architect after he left school, discovering that he had a gift for drawing. An uncle suggested he apply to *L'Ecole des arts décoratifs*, where Pialat first studied architecture in 1944 before turning to painting. While he claimed that he had no real facility, Pialat worked seriously at drawing and painting for three years, completing a *certificat d'études*, and exhibiting work in the Salon for artists under thirty from 1945 to 1947. He took on a variety of jobs, hoping to be able to make enough money to continue painting, but ultimately realised that there was no way that he could support himself and still paint seriously.

> Quand j'ai dû abandonner, ça a été un grand choc – j'avais vingt-et-un ans, je suis devenu représentant, j'ai essayé de continuer la peinture parce que j'avais un peu de temps: en vain. Après cette rupture j'étais complètement malade, je passais ma journée à dormir, je me levais pour déjeuner et je me recouchais. Ça a duré des mois comme ça, j'ai visité la moitié de la France sans rien foutre.[21] (Pialat 1980b: 4)

His depression lasted almost two years and he emerged from it slowly, working in amateur theatre and making films in 16mm. Even

21 'When I had to give it up, it was a tremendous shock – I was twenty-one, I became a sales representative, I tried to keep painting because I had some free time: in vain. When I stopped I was really upset, I spent whole days in bed, getting up for lunch and then going back to sleep. It went on for months like that, I travelled around France without doing any work at all.'

in his seventies, Pialat's regret for the painter he might have been emerged as he talked about a portrait he had painted when he was eighteen (Pialat 2000: 71).

In 1947, Pialat's parents finally gave up their business in Montreuil, its lack of profitability assured by the fact that neither Maurice nor his parents were averse to borrowing from the cash reserves, a fact alluded to in *La Gueule ouverte*. Pialat's parents left him with 18,000 francs to begin life on his own and moved back to Cunlhat (Mérigeau 2002: 29). Pialat attempted to finish his education, taking the *baccalauréat* exam the next year, when he was twenty-three, but just missed a passing score. This failure inevitably seemed to justify his father's reproach that he was lazy, while the fact that he was older than his peers apparently left him with the sense that he was both too old and chronically behind, which pervaded his personal life and his career. 'Quand on a eu une adolescence et des études ratées, on en conserve une amertume,' he told interviewers in 1980[22] (Pialat 1980b: 8).

He married Micheline in 1949, moving to Lyon to take up work as a sales representative, first for a pharmaceutical firm, then for Olivetti. He was growing serious about filmmaking and began to meet others with similar ambitions – deciding finally to move back to Paris. Jean-Louis Trintignant, whom he met in Lyon, would later introduce him to Claude Langmann. Langmann, who was beginning a career as an actor, would become an intimate friend, and Langmann's family (including his sister Arlette, seventeen years Pialat's junior) would become – at least for a time – the close family he had never had.

Pialat dismissed the transitional period which led up to his first full-length film, *L'Enfance nue*, as 'laborieuse' – yet it began with what must have seemed like a lucky break. While he was with Olivetti he spent a month making a short comic film about the company for their New Year's celebration. He showed it, among some other shorts, to the producer Pierre Braunberger, whose eye for talent had led him to produce early work by Jean Renoir. Braunberger (and Truffaut) encouraged Pialat to make the documentary *L'Amour existe*, and financed the filming. It brought Pialat important recognition – and the Prix Jean Vigo – but it did not jump-start his career. He was forced to continue doing small projects: a series of documentary films on

22 'When your adolescent years and your studies go badly, it leaves you with a feeling of bitterness.'

Turkey (evoked in *Nous ne vieillirons pas ensemble*), some work for TV news, a series of films for the Ministry of Foreign Affairs to be shown abroad, some editing and camera work. He and Claude Langmann (who had taken the name Claude Berri) collaborated on a short tragi-comic film about a prostitute, *Janine*, starring Evelyne Ker, for which Berri supplied the script. Pialat admired Berri's gift for dialogue, which he was later to compare to that of Marcel Pagnol whose popularity as a writer and filmmaker he always envied. However, *Janine* never made it past the censors.

Pialat claimed that he did not regret the work he did during this period, but he obviously resented his place outside the charmed circle of young New Wave filmmakers whose early work met with such extraordinary popular success. He was seven years older than Truffaut, but had to wait until 1969, ten years after the triumph of the New Wave and *Les 400 Coups*, before he was able to find financing for *L'Enfance nue* – that same year he made a brief appearance, playing the part of the police commissioner, in what was New Wave director Claude Chabrol's twentieth film *Que la bête meure* (*This Man Must Die*).

Beyond this point Pialat's career becomes a kind of cinematic lifework, where the people closest to him are involved both in his life and in his films. His first wife, Micheline, to whom he was married for twenty years, remained an important supporter, briefly managing his production company, *Les Films du Livradois*. If her affection for him is suggested by the unusual role of advocate assumed by the wife in *Nous ne vieillirons pas ensemble*, her continuing presence in his life was signalled by the character of Micheline in *Le Garçu*, some twenty years later. It would be the same for Arlette Langmann, who played a crucial role in his work through seven films (including *La Maison des bois*). Sylvie Danton, whom he married in 1987, collaborated with him on the scenario for three films beginning with *Police* in 1985 and culminating in *Le Garçu* ten years later. This film, Pialat's last, focuses on the complicated family relationships surrounding the four-year-old Antoine, played by their son, Antoine Pialat. Pialat's belated fatherhood – he was sixty-six when Antoine was born – and the fact that his final film focuses primarily on the relationship between a father and a son, his own son, draws attention both to the importance of children in his films and to the crucial issue of paternity in his conception of himself as an artist.

L'Amour existe: a sense of place

The film that first brought Pialat professional recognition, the twenty-one minute black and white documentary film about *la banlieue* ('the suburbs,' marginal areas outside the city) entitled *L'Amour existe*, provides a telling perspective on his later films and an introduction to what will become major themes in his work. *L'Amour existe* builds on Pialat's previous documentary experience, but moves beyond documentary to autobiography, fusing a highly personal, poetic voice-over commentary (although Pialat does not do the voice-over) with documentary images.

The opening images, preceding and running behind the credits – the Saint-Lazare station, a high angle shot of people moving in the crush of the crowd up and down the steps in the Métro, others moving in a long line towards the Métro entrance in the rain; people packed in Métro cars, glimpses of buses and cars caught in rush-hour traffic – establish what will be a recurrent motif: the various means of loco-motion that define the suburbs by their exclusion from the city centre. The *banlieusard*, or suburban dweller, if not retired, inevitably becomes a commuter.

The first words of the voice-over commentary connect this visual motif to an autobiographical 'Souvenir' (the title of the first section) that is none other than Pialat's earliest recollection of passing trains: 'Mon premier souvenir est un souvenir de banlieue. Très loin dans ma mémoire, un train de banlieue passe, comme dans un film. La mémoire et les films se remplissent d'objets qu'on ne pourra plus appréhender'[23] (Pialat 1962: 48). What follows is an autobiographical narrative that confirms the powerful impress of the years in Courbevoie, a boyhood and adolescence darkened and constrained by the war and the Occupation. The winter brought Panzers on manoeuvres to the bois de Vincennes, the streets are silent, in the spring and summer *guinguettes* (open-air cafés) are shuttered, 'les baignades de la Marne dorment dans la boue'.[24] Piaf's lyrics sum up the general impression: 'La banlieue triste qui s'ennuie, défile grise sous la pluie'.[25]

23 'My earliest recollection is a memory of the suburbs. In a distant memory, a suburban train passes, as in a film. Memory and films fill up with objects whose meaning we can no longer grasp.'
24 'swimming-holes on the Marne River sleep in the mud'.
25 'the sad boring suburbs go by in the rain'.

Black and white images – of buildings, boutiques, the entrance to a train station, of children getting water from a fountain, a girl on a bicycle – provide more impersonal, fleeting glimpses of the landscape evoked by the narrative. Like Blaise Cendrars and Robert Doisneau's 1949 portrayal of *La banlieue de Paris* as a poverty-stricken landscape, a 'paysage pauvre', Pialat's film is firmly anchored in a sense of class difference. However, Pialat's *banlieue* lacks the energy and hope of the post-war period that characterised their work. Instead, an almost Proustian melancholy and nostalgia pervade 'Souvenir'. The voice-over narrative, paralleled by a long tracking shot, concludes: 'les chateaux de l'enfance s'éloignent, des adultes reviennent dans la cour de leur école – comme à la récréation – puis des trains les emportent'.[26] With this evocation of trains the first section reconnects with the initial image of the Saint Lazare Station, but not without suggesting both the terror of deportation and the fact that there is an inevitable and perhaps abrupt end to childhood, and to life's journey. Yet unlike Proust, Pialat remains uncertain whether art can preserve what would otherwise be lost: 'Memory and films fill up with objects whose meaning we can no longer grasp'. The film – like the title *L'Amour existe*, which has no explicit connection either to the narrative or the images themselves – becomes an affirmation in the face of Pialat's own doubts, both a gesture of defiance and a form of self-assertion.

This first section establishes the narrator's identity and credibility as a witness, while the next three sections present his observations, dividing the *banlieue* into three possible classes of habitation: *le pavillon, le HLM, les bidonvilles* ('the detached house, subsidised housing, shanty towns'), each one representing a greater degree of poverty and marginality. Only the first, *le pavillon*, retains the earliest associations of the *banlieue* with the countryside outside the city walls, offering – after years of scrimping and saving – the promise of a rural retreat or retirement home. The next section shows this refuge, and the countryside as well, threatened by its subdivision into zones destined for urbanisation and quickly overbuilt with shoddily constructed high rises touted as a solution to the post-war housing crisis. Yet even these zones are encroached upon by *bidonvilles* whose Spanish, Italian, Portuguese and North African immigrants throw

26 'childhood castles fade into the distance, adults come back to their old school playground – as though for recess – then trains take them away'.

together shacks of planks and tar paper so flammable that they periodically self-destruct, the smoke and flames providing Pialat with a fade to black to conclude the sequence.

The 'Statistics' of the next section give numerical values to the social and cultural poverty of the area, while the final section ,'Calme', takes up the plight of the retired: 'Le repos à neuf mille francs par mois. L'isolement dans les vieux quartiers. L'Asile'.[27] The film concludes by evoking 'un enfant doué' (a gifted child) who might have grown up to express the beauty of suburban streets had he not remained isolated and alone. This unidentified 'gifted child' becomes the youthful counterpart of the narrator in the first section, but the child is also an abstraction of the many images of children in the film. The most powerful of these is the one the camera approaches most closely, a small boy sitting on what appears to be an unmade bed in a cluttered *bidonville* shack. He is crying, although the voice-over covers the sound, and his shoulders shake with sobs as he turns his tear-stained face towards the camera advancing toward him.

This crying child is emblematic of the current of irreparable damage and loss that runs through Pialat's cinema, but rarely is the reason for this damage or loss made as clear or anchored in a social reality that explains it so completely. All of the characteristic elements of Pialat's work are visible in this film: his attraction to documentary, the autobiographical substratum of his work, his identification with the working class – the people he referred to as 'les gens qui prennent le métro' (people who take the subway) – his portrayal of the sadness, pain and loneliness of those who, for whatever reason, are forgotten or excluded, relegated to the margins of society (Pialat 1979: 49). His refusal of the picturesque and his unwillingness to look away from the more sordid aspects of his subject suggest why critics would later label his work 'naturalist'.

Although the film contains powerful elements of social criticism, it is typical of Pialat's work that this criticism never coalesces into an attack, a denunciation or any overtly political statement. In this case the film ends with a plea directed at humanity in general: 'il ne doit rien rester qui perpétue la misère'.[28] Here, as in his later films, Pialat reserves judgement, portraying all of the complexities of his characters

27 'Rest at nine thousand francs a month. Isolation in ageing neighborhoods. The old people's home.'
28 'nothing should remain to perpetuate misery and poverty'.

and the situations in which they find themselves. In fact, the final images of *L'amour existe* demonstrate a painterly awareness of the way a composition changes when it is seen from different vantage points. The last images show a statue whose raised arm, lifted in triumph, can be read as a gesture of entreaty when viewed from a different angle – a curious commentary, at a distance of more than twenty years, on Pialat's gesture of victory at Cannes.

The next chapter will take up Pialat's efforts to find his place as a filmmaker in relation to the two major (and contradictory) influences on his work: the popular Saturday night cinema of his adolescence and the *Nouvelle Vague*.

References

Assayas, Olivier and C. Denis, C. Kahn, N. Lvovsky (1998), 'Quelques Vagues plus tard', *Cahiers du cinéma*, no. hors série.

Bergala, Alain (1983), 'Maurice Pialat, un marginal du centre', *Cahiers du cinéma*, no. 354.

Bonitzer, Pascal (1981), 'Le Rayonnement Maurice Pialat', *Cahiers du cinéma*, nos. 323–4.

Bonnaire, Sandrine (2003), 'Témoignage', *Cahiers du cinéma*, no. 576.

Beugnet, Martine (2003), 'Nouveau réalisme et politique de l'anti-spectacle', *French Studies* 57: 3 349–66.

Breillat, Catherine (1992), 'Portrait d'un homme qu'on aime pour ses défauts', in *Maurice Pialat, l'enfant sauvage*, Turin, Museo National del cinema.

Bresson, Robert (1957), 'Propos de Robert Bresson', *Cahiers du cinéma*, no. 13.

Cendrars, Blaise and Robert Doisneau (1949, reprint 1966), *La Banlieue de Paris*, Paris, Seghers.

De Baecque, Antoine (1992), 'Pialat, l'emmerdeur' in *Maurice Pialat, l'enfant sauvage* Torino, Museo Nationale del cinema.

De Baecque, Antoine and Thierry Jousse (1996), *Retour du cinéma*, Paris, Hatier.

Depardieu, Gérard (1988), *Lettres volées*, Lausanne, Editions J-C Lattès.

Duras, Marguérite (1997), 'Au hasard Balthazar' in *Robert Bresson: Eloge*, Milan/Paris, Mazzota/Cinémathèque française.

Dutronc, Jacques (2000), 'Je suis celui qui traverse', *Cahiers du cinéma*, no. 551.

Gonzalez, Christian (1985), *Gérard Depardieu*, Paris, Edilig.

Magny, Joël (1991), 'Le Geste de Pialat', *Cahiers du cinéma*, no. 449.

Magny, Joël (1992), *Maurice Pialat*, Paris, Cahiers du cinéma.

Mérigeau, Pascal (2002), *Pialat*, Paris, Editions Grasset & Fasquelle.

Oudart, Jean-Pierre (1972), 'Le Hors-champ de l'auteur', *Cahiers du cinéma*, nos. 236–7.

Pialat, Maurice (1962), 'L'Amour existe' in *Avant-Scène du cinéma*, no. 12.

Pialat, Maurice (1979), 'Entretien', *Cinématographe*, no. 50.

Pialat, Maurice (1979b), 'Entretien', *Cahiers du cinéma*, no. 304

Pialat, Maurice (1980), 'Entretien', *Cinématographe*, no. 57.

Pialat, Maurice (1980b), 'Entretien', *Positif*, no. 235.

Pialat, Maurice (1983), 'Entretien', *Cinématographe*, no. 94.

Pialat, Maurice (1984), *A nos amours: scénario et dialogue du film*, Paris, L'Herminier.

Pialat, Maurice (1995), 'Entretien', *Positif*, no. 418.

Pialat, Maurice (2000), 'Entretien: sur la colère', *Cahiers du cinéma*, no. 550.

Reader, Keith (2000), *Robert Bresson*, Manchester/New York, Manchester University Press.

Sontag, Susan (1966), 'Spiritual Style in the Films of Robert Bresson' in *Against Interpretation*, New York, Farrar Straus Giroux.

Trémois, Claude-Marie (1974), 'Le Nouveau Naturel (3)' *Télérama*.

2

Pialat and the *Nouvelle Vague*

'Vous savez, *j'en veux* (je dis bien: j'en veux) à la Nouvelle Vague',[1] Pialat announced abruptly during an a 1979 interview with *Cahiers du Cinéma* – the very journal that had served as a seedbed for the New Wave some twenty years earlier (Pialat 1979: 15). The interviewers parried the thrust by expressing surprise at his antagonism and claiming that he actually had much in common with the *Nouvelle Vague*. Pialat did not deny it, but insisted: 'C'était si on veut le lièvre et la tortue: ils faisaient des films et je n'en faisais pas (j'étais pourtant plus vieux qu'eux). La Nouvelle Vague, c'était une histoire de copains et quand on n'en était pas, on avait du mal à tourner'[2] (Pialat 1979: 14).

Pialat's outburst reflected his longstanding resentment over the fact that the young directors of the *Nouvelle Vague* had already begun to make names for themselves in the 1960s while he was still struggling to make films. His sense that he had not been given the same opportunities as the little group of friends at *Cahiers* led him to reject the *Nouvelle Vague* and belittle its importance. He turned elsewhere to find a model for a successful career in film, looking back to the popular cinema of the 1930s and 1940s, to films by major directors such as Pagnol, Carné or Renoir and the Saturday night cinema he had loved as a child. Yet the small-budget revolution associated with the *Nouvelle Vague* made it increasingly difficult for

---

1 'You know, *I'm angry* (I mean it: I'm angry) with the *Nouvelle Vague*.'
2 'You might say that it was the tortoise and the hare: they were making films and I wasn't (although I was older than they were). The New Wave was all about a group of friends and when you weren't part of it, you had trouble making films.'

any filmmaker to aspire to a career in the mould of Pagnol or Carné. Somewhat extravagantly, Pialat blamed the *Nouvelle Vague* both for his own delayed beginnings in film as well as for the decline of the popular cinema he had loved as a child.

Yet Pialat's continuing allegiance to an older *cinéma de papa* denounced by Truffaut was difficult to reconcile with his own practice as a filmmaker and his desire to be recognised as an author in New Wave terms. Pialat's profound ambivalence toward the *Nouvelle Vague* was one of the defining elements of his career. This ambivalence emerged with particular poignancy in his last interview with Charles Tesson of *Cahiers* in October 2000. During the interview Tesson wondered aloud whether: 'Ce que la Nouvelle Vague a dit, c'est vous qui l'avez fait, ce n'est pas eux, si l'on se rapporte à leurs intentions'.[3] Surprisingly, Pialat did not object, or attempt to denigrate the *Nouvelle Vague*, replying instead: 'Vous êtes bien gentil. Est-ce que vous l'écririez? Vous le laisserez?'[4] (Pialat 2000: 68).

This chapter considers Pialat's place within the context of French cinema history, focusing on his relationship to the *Nouvelle Vague* and to two major filmmakers of the 1930s and 1940s (to some degree themselves opposing models) against whose work Pialat measured his own: Jean Renoir and Marcel Carné.

The group at *Cahiers*

Truffaut initially denied that the *Nouvelle Vague* was either a movement, a school or a group, maintaining in a famous quip that 'Je ne vois qu'un point commun entre les jeunes cinéastes: ils pratiquent tous assez systématiquement l'appareil à sous, contrairement aux vieux metteurs en scène qui préfèrent les cartes et le whiskey'.[5] (Marie 1997: 25). Whether movement, group or school, the *Nouvelle Vague* has been defined both narrowly – limiting it to the small group of cinephiles and critics associated with André Bazin at *Cahiers du*

---

3 'What the New Wave said, you are the one who did it, instead of them, if we consider what they intended.'

4 'You are very kind. Would you write that? Will you leave it in [the interview]?'

5 'I only see only one thing the younger filmmakers have in common, they all play pinball pretty regularly in contrast to old filmmakers who prefer cards and whisky.'

cinéma: Claude Chabrol, François Truffaut, Jean-Luc Godard, Eric Rohmer, Jacques Rivette (Frodon 1995: 24), sometimes including Pierre Kast and Jacques Doniol-Valcroze (Marie 1997: 43) – and more broadly, to include what was called 'le nouveau cinéma' (new cinema) to distinguish it from the group at *Cahiers*. The 'nouveau cinéma': Alain Resnais, Chris Marker, Jacques Demy, Agnès Varda and Louis Malle (to which some historians might add François Reichenbach or the ethnologist Jean Rouch) was more likely to approach filmmaking through the *court-métrage* or the documentary (Jeancolas 1979: 113–21; Frodon 1995: 46; De Baecque 1998: 97). Film historian René Prédal lists thirteen 'founding films' of the New Wave, including Rouch's *Moi, un noir* and Jacques Rozier's *Adieu Philippine* (Prédal 1996: 160). However, Pialat's ire, when he targeted the *Nouvelle Vague*, was focused exclusively on the critics of *Cahiers* whom he disparaged as bourgeois, aesthetes and snobs (Pialat 1979: 9).

However, as Alain Bergala points out, rather than being elitist, the critics of *Cahiers* hoped to persuade the general public to think about film differently (Bergala 1998: 36). Godard celebrated the success of François Truffaut's *Les Quatre Cents Coups* and Alain Resnais' *Hiroshima mon amour* at the Cannes Film Festival in 1959 as the first steps towards victory over the ambitious studio productions – generally literary adaptations – that regularly won the prizes at Cannes, Venice and elsewhere. Truffaut contrasted such work, which he ironically baptised the 'tradition of quality', with that of filmmakers who belonged, in his estimation, to an entirely different category: *un cinéma d'auteurs*. 'Il s'agit de Jean Renoir, Robert Bresson, Jean Cocteau, Jacques Becker, Abel Gance, Max Ophuls, Jacques Tati, Roger Leenhardt ... ce sont des auteurs qui écrivent souvent leur dialogue et quelques-uns inventent eux-mêmes les histoires qu'ils mettent en scène'[6] (Marie 1997: 35). Truffaut argued that a new generation of filmmakers should make films differently: 'il faut filmer autre chose, avec un autre esprit et d'autres méthodes'[7] (Prédal 1996: 156). However, as René Prédal argues, the aesthetic revolution Truffaut had in mind would not have been possible without 'the small budget revolution' (Prédal 1996: 151). After Chabrol's success – and the success of Truffaut's *Quatre Cents Coups* and Godard's *A bout de*

6 'It is filmmakers such as Jean Renoir [...] who are authors, who write their own dialogue, and some of them invent the stories they film.'

7 'you have to film other things, with another mindset and other methods'.

souffle in quick succession – producers opened their doors to aspiring filmmakers, many of whom, like the group at *Cahiers*, had no real experience in filmmaking, but whose willingness to make films on a shoestring budget created the potential for large profit margins.

The small-budget revolution was already under way when Pialat began *L'Amour existe*. However, his own approach to the medium mirrored that of the 'nouveau cinéma' – he tried to gain professional experience and mastery of the medium, beginning with a short documentary and expecting it to lead, as it did for Jacques Demy or Alain Resnais, to full-length feature films. However, when no opportunities materialised, despite the success of *L'Amour existe*, Pialat held the New Wave responsible, deploring the success of Truffaut's attack on the studio system of the 1950s and 'quality films' precisely because it opened the doors of the profession to a host of inexperienced directors whose projects competed for limited funding. Throughout his career, Pialat remained attached to a certain idea of professionalism grounded in studio filmmaking where ample budgets would allow for doing period films or undertaking ambitious projects. He insisted that 'un des drames en France, depuis l'avènement de la *Nouvelle Vague*, c'est qu'on refait éternellement son premier film, il n'y a pas d'épanouissement'[8] (Pialat 1987: 62). Yet he conceded that even when he did have more generous budgets he did not approach making films differently and rarely used the money to full advantage. The tension between Pialat's belief in the value of large-budget studio productions and his own cinematic practice, far closer to that of the New Wave, explains the contradictions of his assessment of two important predecessors: Jean Renoir and Marcel Carné.

Carné versus Renoir

Carné, the demanding, controlling, sometimes tyrannical director whose artistry is reflected in extraordinary studio productions, might in some ways be considered the precursor of the 1950s 'tradition of quality' (or *cinéma de papa*) with its carefully wrought literary scenarios, important stars and lavish period recreations – all filmed with a

---

8 'one of the worst things in France, since the arrival of the New Wave, is that you are endlessly redoing your first film, there is no development'.

technical expertise that created an illusion of reality based on an apparently seamless narrative continuity. Carné's last great film, the 1945 *Les Enfants du Paradis*, was a hugely ambitious project that involved recreating 'the acrobatics, sideshows, vaudevilles, and dramas performed along the Boulevard du Temple during the regimes of Charles X and Louis Philippe'. Major stars: Arletty, Jean-Louis Barrault, Pierre Brasseur and Maria Casarès, took the primary roles; the Paris Conservatory Orchestra recorded the music for the film, and the entire Boulevard du Temple was reconstructed in three different sets requiring 67,500 hours of labour (Turk 1989: 221, 224).

By contrast, Jean Renoir began filming what is considered his masterpiece, the 1939 *La Règle du jeu,* without even having finished the scenario. Nor did Renoir opt for well-known actors, even playing the key role of Octave himself. Unlike Carné, Renoir preferred to film in natural surroundings, convinced that the film's setting had a powerful effect on his actors. He took risks in filming Jean Gabin and Carette on real trains in *La Bête humaine,* and considerably depleted what had initially been a very ample budget by renting a real chateau in Sologne for *La Règle du jeu.* Unlike Carné, who rarely deviated from his written scenario, Renoir allowed discoveries and new insights to take a film in different and unexpected directions – 'le sujet vous boulotte, on est attiré et on tourne malgré soi des choses qu'on n'avait jamais prévues parce qu'elles appartiennent au sujet'[9] (Chevrie 1992: 74).

Pialat's ambition to practise film as an art and as an auteur, his willingness to work with inexperienced or amateur actors, the importance he attributed to improvisation, his reluctance to create, or follow, a detailed scenario, and his personal connection to the films he made – his participation as writer, actor and in some cases producer – all link him to the New Wave and to Renoir. Yet, after having seen Renoir's *Le Crime de Monsieur Lange* in a retrospective at the Cinémathèque, Pialat was also quick to criticise Renoir's technique: 'je trouvais qu'il tournait certains plans comme un cochon, alors que Carné, que je n'ai jamais vraiment aimé, tournait "bien". Il n'empêche que Renoir tourne infiniment mieux que Carné dont *Les Enfants du Paradis* est considéré comme "le plus grand film français", du moins

9 'the subject eats at you, you're drawn in and in spite of yourself you film things you never planned to because they belong to the subject'.

c'est le jugement des Césars'[10] (Chevrie 1992: 73). His own preference went to *La Bête humaine*. Pialat's enthusiasm for Renoir's adaptation of Zola's novel never waned: 'Chaque fois que je vois *La Bête humaine*, j'ai huit ans. Le jour où je n'aimerai plus *La Bête humaine*, alors là!'[11] (Pialat 2000: 68) Yet as Marc Chevrie points out, Pialat's judgment about the film: 'C'est un film complètement de Renoir qui est quand même un peu tourné comme un film de Carné'[12] represents his ideal: a Renoir film done by Carné (Chevrie 1992: 74).

Much of Pialat's criticism of his own work – scenarios he considered too diffuse, vague or poorly constructed; films with weak or missing transitions; technical difficulties – stems from his admiration for the well-made film *à la* Carné as an artisanal ideal. What he denigrates as his deficiencies are the formal consequences of a more Renoirian approach to filmmaking: 'Ce que j'essaye d'obtenir, Pialat explained, 'c'est de créer, en accord avec les comédiens, à partir d'une situation donnée dont on peut s'écarter en cours de tournage'[13] (Pialat 1974: 6). Although Pialat persisted in envisioning the successful filmmaker as a popular director in the mode of Pagnol or Carné, he admitted ruefully 'j'ai quand même été trop marqué par le cinéma d'auteur, les restes de la *Nouvelle Vague*, pour qu'il n'y en ait pas de traces, ça ne s'en ira jamais'[14] (Pialat 1985: 19).

In fact, it is possible to list something that Pialat shares with almost all of the *Cahiers* group. Like Truffaut's Antoine Doinel series, Pialat's films are a form of autobiography – and both Truffaut and Pialat seek the kind of personal involvement in their stories that leads them, like Renoir, to risk playing crucial roles in their own films. With Godard, Pialat shares the willingness to break the rules of classical filmmaking. With Rohmer, whose carefully plotted studies of the desires, pretensions and foibles of bourgeois couples seem at a

10 'I thought that he filmed certain shots like a pig, while Carné, whom I've never really liked, shot them "well". All the same, Renoir's films are infinitely better than Carné's whose *Les Enfants du Paradis* is considered "the greatest French film" at least if you go by the Césars [awards]'.
11 'Every time I see *La Bête humaine* I'm eight years old again. The day I don't love *La Bête humaine* any more, well!'
12 'It's a completely Renoir film done a little like a film by Carné'.
13 'What I try to do, with the actors' consent, is to create something by beginning with a set situation that we can deviate from in the course of the shoot'.
14 'all the same I've been too influenced by auteurist cinema, what remains of the *Nouvelle Vague*, for that not to have left its mark, that will never go away'.

considerable remove from Pialat's universe, Pialat shares both an interest in provincial settings and a very personal kind of formal rigour. With Jacques Rivette, Pialat shares a background in theatre and the desire to probe the relationship between life and art.

An anti-Chabrol

In this litany of New Wave filmmakers whose work has features in common with Pialat, Chabrol figures as something of an exception; his work throws into relief some of the fundamental differences that separate Pialat from the *Nouvelle Vague*. While Chabrol's cinema is associated primarily with a genre, the thriller, or detective film, and a milieu, the bourgeoisie, Pialat's work has little affinity with either. The New Wave's fascination with Hollywood directors and genres, particularly gangster and B-series films, has no counterpart in Pialat's films. Not that the westerns of Pialat's childhood or the popularity of the thriller as a genre did not tempt him – 'Qui n'a pas rêvé de tourner un polar? un western? Moi, j'en rêve en tous cas, et depuis longtemps' (Pialat 1979b: 64) ('Who hasn't dreamed of making a detective film? A western? I have in any case, and for a long time') Pialat enthused in an interview in the late 1970s. Yet he concentrated solely on subjects that resonated with his own experience until the mid-1980s when he made *Police*. However, even *Police* was conceived in terms that eliminated most of the genre's characteristic elements. The film was a critical success, if not a popular one, but it was an experience Pialat did not repeat. Although his next two productions were also ostensibly in traditional genres: his adaptation of Bernanos's novel *Sous le Soleil de Satan* and his biopic: *Van Gogh*, both films undermine these genres even as they reinforce Pialat's deep connection to a French cultural context.

It is possible to stretch a point and draw a parallel between Chabrol's criminal portraits of the bourgeoisie and Pialat's dislike for his own class. This dislike surfaces in *Loulou*, where Isabelle Huppert's Nelly abandons her bourgeois husband to live with a *loubard*, and again in *A nos amours* where Pialat's character, a furrier, berates his son's bourgeois brother-in-law for being more interested in money than talent. However, while Chabrol's most important work demonstrates his ambivalent fascination with his own class, Pialat avoided subjects set in bourgeois milieus: 'Il faut regarder les gens qu'on aime. Quand je tourne sur la classe bourgeoise cela sonne faux; je ne me sens pas à l'aise avec des gens que je n'aime pas'[15] (Pialat 1979b: 61). Like Carné, whose father was a cabinetmaker, Pialat valued the warmth and openness of working-class people: 'Je suis plus proche d'eux parce qu'ils sont de contact facile. Il n'y a pas là de barrières, culturelles ou autres. On rentre dans un bistrot, on parle à un type du peuple dans la minute qui suit. Le rapport est évident'[16] (Pialat 1980: 8).

Pialat also avoids the classic New Wave setting: Paris. Although *A nos amours*, *Loulou*, *Police* and much of *Le Garçu* are set in Paris, the city itself is largely absent. There are none of the valentines to Paris that correspond to the exhilarating tour offered to the provincial cousin during a wild ride in his city cousin's convertible in Chabrol's *Les Cousins*, or the magic moment between day and twilight when the streetlights come on in *A bout de souffle*, or even the many shots of the Eiffel Tower that accompany the opening credits of *Les Quatre Cents Coups*. Pialat's preference goes instead to working-class and provincial settings more reminiscent of the populist cinema of the thirties. However, perhaps the profound connection and crucial differences between Pialat and the New Wave come through most clearly in a comparison between Pialat's and Truffaut's first full-length films.

Les Quatre Cents Coups and *L'Enfance nue* (*Naked childhood*)

As Joël Magny points out, Alan Williams' history of French film, *Republic of Images*, dismissed *L'Enfance nue* as a *Nouvelle Vague*-style chronicle of adolescence, one of the many films about children inspired by *Les Quatre Cents Coups* (Magny 1992: 11). There are certainly obvious and striking parallels between the two films – beginning with the fact that both films focus on a young boy whose misbehaviour and family difficulties escalate to the point that he is turned over to the police and sent to the equivalent of a centre for delinquent minors.

---

15 'You have to look at people you like. When I film the middle class it rings false; I don't feel at ease with people I don't like.'
16 'I am closer to them because they are approachable. There aren't any barriers, cultural or otherwise. You go into a bar, a minute later you are talking to a working-class guy, the rapport is obvious.'

Both stories end ambiguously, with the famous freeze frame of Antoine Doinel at the shore in Truffaut's case; or in Pialat's film with the wrenching letter from François to his foster parents in which he expresses the hope that he will be able to visit them at Christmas. Both filmmakers considered their work to have a documentary dimension and both films were made on slender budgets. Both films were shot on location, Truffaut's in Paris, Pialat's in the northern mining country around Lens, using relatively unknown or non-professional actors. Both filmmakers even had the same impulse to salvage otherwise unusable footage by having it serve as the background to the opening credits. Yet a closer look at the two films suggests Pialat's more radical realism, which links him to Jean Rouch and Jacques Rozier.

Truffaut's desire to make a film that resembled a documentary without being one, reflected his admiration for the neo-realism of Rossellini, despite his avowed preference for fiction over documentary: 'ce qui m'a amené au cinéma, c'est la fiction et ... je ne désire pas changer mon point de vue là-dessus' (Truffaut 1988: 105) ('What attracted me to film, is fiction and ... I have no desire to change my view on that'). However, Truffaut's preference for fiction equates primarily to an attachment to narrative, to storytelling – 'elle [la fiction] est dans la façon d'agencer les choses, de présenter le récit comme une narration, un conte, et non pas comme la relation neutre d'une chose'[17] (Truffaut 1988: 105). In this sense Truffaut's approach to filmmaking does not differ radically from that of 'quality' filmmakers. The film tells the story of his main character, Antoine Doinel, who is at the centre of the action from the beginning through to the final frame of the film (Holmes and Ingram 1998: 116). Truffaut allows the viewer to understand Antoine's situation by providing a series of telling exchanges between Antoine and each of his parents as well as his best friend René. Point-of-view shots (such as the view of his mother kissing a stranger) allow the viewer to take in events as Antoine himself does and ultimately, through the device of the interview with the psychiatrist at the detention centre, the viewer is allowed direct insight into Antoine's thoughts and feelings that clarifies any confusion about his earlier behaviour. Truffaut avoids a flat or neutral presentation of events by creating moments of dramatic tension and

17 'The fiction is in the way things are organised, the presentation of the events as a narrative, a story, and not a neutral account of things'.

détente, even drawing inspiration from Hitchcock on how to edit a sequence in order to obtain the maximum suspense (Truffaut 1988: 100).

By contrast, Pialat's film was conceived as a documentary and based on a year of research in which he had the cooperation of *l'Assistance sociale* in the area around Lens and Arras. Inspired by the early Lumière films that he had seen just before beginning the filming, he claimed that 'en tournant *L'Enfance nue*, je pensais au *Goûter de Bébé*' (Pialat 1974: 5) ('While shooting *L'Enfance nue*, I was thinking about *Baby's Tea Time*'). His choice of Lumière as a model is also emblematic of his desire for a realist cinema freed from commercial constraints and narrative conventions, relying for its effects on the camera's particular way of capturing and reproducing the real. In fact when he was asked how he introduced fictional elements into the documentary material, Pialat dismissed the question, claiming 'la fiction en l'occurence c'est peu de chose, c'est simplet' ('the fiction in this case is hardly anything, it's simplistic') and claimed that the film had taken shape on the set during the fifteen days of filming (Pialat 1980: 4). Pialat's decision to focus on the character of François was no doubt crucial to his recasting the film as fiction. However, by shaping his story out of documentary material rather than conceiving his film in terms of a story about his characters, he reverses the relationship between documentary and fiction operative in Truffaut's film. This suggests as much of a debt to the Jean Rouch of *Moi, un noir* – whose actors played themselves living their lives in front of the camera – as to Truffaut.

Pialat's fidelity to his medium leads him to reject the kind of aesthetic concerns that caused Truffaut to downplay potentially depressing, ugly or sordid elements of his story. In fact, Pialat considered the photography of *L'Enfance nue* successful precisely because it rendered the ugly colours and harsh contrasts of the setting (Pialat 1974: 3). He was no less stringent in dealing with his characters. Troubled, closed and hostile, François lacks the impish charm of Antoine Doinel. He steals and lies, constantly wets his bed, and throws his sister Josette's cat down the stairwell, torn at the last minute between trying to nurse it back to health and deciding to finish it off. 'Ton chat ... coiiic' he finally tells her, drawing a finger across his throat. And in the final gesture that costs him his place in his second foster family, he joins a gang of boys throwing metal railroad pins at cars from an overpass and causes an accident. The film's dramatic relief stems more from the feelings of uneasiness, sadness, discomfort or dismay provoked by François's behaviour than from any effort on Pialat's part to structure the narrative in order to create suspense or *détente*.

In fact, the beginning of *L'Enfance nue* suggests several different narratives and their connections are not established until well into the film. The opening credits run against images of a union rally. Drummers and men in uniform pass by the camera (generally stationary, *à la* Lumière). The marchers carry signs: 'Pour le plein emploi', 'une vie décente' ('For full employment', 'a decent life'). Only the sound of the drums accompanies the credits, and as the sound fades an older man's voice is heard: 'Tu vois, j'aurais pu être menuiser' ('You see? I could have been a cabinetmaker') followed by a boy's voice 'c'était ton métier?' ('that was your job?') and the answer 'non, à la mine j'étais aiguilleur' ('no, at the mine I was a switchman'). The disjunction between the rally and the voice-over is all the more disorienting in that neither has any obvious connection to the first image of the film – a shot in which a young boy tries on a suit jacket, framed by a saleswoman and another woman, ostensibly his mother, who puts her hand on his shoulder. The union rally does not pre-figure events in the story, or provide a political context for what happens in the film and the voice-over will not be contextualised until the second half of the film. Yet this beginning does implicitly establish a larger social context in which issues of work (and money), class and family frame the portrayal of 'l'enfance nue' (naked childhood).

The sense of disjunction and discontinuity that characterises the opening credits is carried over into several loosely linked scenes that introduce François, his foster parents (Simone and Robert 'Robby' Joigny), and their daughter Josette. Nothing in these scenes allows the viewer to see that Simone is gradually reaching the decision – as she subsequently tells the director of social services – that 'ce n'est plus possible avec François' ('it is no longer possible with François'). Simone merely buys her 'son' a jacket, Robby buys his daughter a record. When they stop in a local café, Josette asks her father for a franc and he asks François to go up to the counter to buy his cigarettes, then lets him keep the change. Pialat neither explains nor emphasises, counting on the viewer to notice that François rips a watch off a counter display while waiting to pay for the cigarettes –

and to note that Josette got the franc that she asked for, while François was merely allowed to keep the change. François, the younger, more fragile child sits across the table from Robby, almost at the edge of the frame, while Josette sits close to her father. Yet this early marginal-isation of François, who, like Antoine Doinel, has no room of his own (he sleeps on the landing at the Joignys') prefigures his rejection by his foster parents.

The film is built up out of a succession of self-contained sequences not always clearly linked – either thematically, psychologically or by cause and effect – but which produce their effect by accretion. The first of three segments of unequal length focuses on the final days, perhaps weeks, (characteristically, the timeframe is unclear) of François's stay with the Joignys. The second section follows François in transit with a group of young children who are being conveyed to an adoption centre. François is largely absent from this section, which focuses on a baby named Vincent who is chosen by prospective foster parents. The final, and longest, section, slightly more than half of the film, is devoted to François's new placement with an elderly couple, 'les Thierry', Pépère and Mémère (played by René and Marie Louise Thierry). The Thierrys have grown children and are grandparents themselves, but have already taken in another foster child, Raoul, somewhat older than the ten-year-old François, in addition to caring for Madame Thierry's very elderly Mother, Mémère-la-vieille.

As this suggests, François is not always at the centre of the narrative, but even when he is, he remains almost as opaque to the viewer as he does to his exasperated foster parents. 'On ne sait pas ce qui passe dans sa tête' ('You don't know what is going on in his head') as Robby points out. Faithful to his character, who is unable to articulate his anger and ambivalence, Pialat conveys François's isolation and the intensity of his unspoken feelings through the composition of the images. A case in point is the sequence consisting solely of François sitting at a table with Josette, the two engaged in a game. Josette, dressed in white, dominates the shot, while François is partly cut off by the frame at the extreme left edge. At the centre of the visual field is a large black cat sitting on Josette's lap. It engages her attention, purring loudly as she pets it, licking her neck, making her laugh and distracting her from the game. François fiddles briefly with the watch on his wrist as he waits for his turn to throw the dice. Then the sequence ends as he insists he has won. François's marginal position in the frame and the fact that Josette is the central figure, preferred by the camera and the cat, makes his claim ring hollow. The next sequence – entirely without dialogue – is devoted to François's destruction of the stolen watch. Pialat frames François standing next to a toilet, holding the watch and scratching the side of the case on the wall, then beating the watch on the rim of the toilet. Finally he positions it on the rim in order to smash it with his foot, but misses, sending it splashing into the toilet bowl. The sequence ends as he flushes the toilet.

Later in the film, once François has been placed with the Thierrys, there are images that show him in a closer physical and emotional proximity to a larger and more accepting family: the kiss he gives Pépère after hearing his war stories, the photograph he takes of Mémère-la-vieille at a wedding reception, the scene in which he stands behind Mémère-la-vieille's chair leaning over her, his head touching hers as she sings 'mon père m'a donné un mari, mon Dieu quel homme, quel petit homme' ('My father gave me a husband, my God what a man, what a little man'). Yet the number of scenes in which François joins in the action are outnumbered by those that isolate him, or show him at the margins of a group or of the image. Pialat captures François in different, often contradictory moments, providing a succession of portraits from which the viewer must draw his or her own conclusions.

After the sudden death of Mémère-la-vieille, François loses his most important connection to the family, and his association with a gang of older boys will lead to his arrest. The concluding sequences of the film focus on the Thierrys, and Raoul, who – perhaps in response to François's absence – has reverted to earlier more problematic behaviour, disappearing for two days with no explanation. Despite the director's efforts to get Raoul to confide in him, the boy never gives a satisfactory explanation for his running away. He might have attempted to make good on an earlier remark to François: 'Moi, j'attendrai pas ma carte d'identité pour savoir d'où je suis né. Je fais mon enquête moi-même'.[18] However, the film gives no more insight into Raoul's motivations than François's and the final section reflects the perplexity of adults faced with troubled children.

18 'I'm not waiting for my identity card to know where I came from. I'm doing my own investigation.'

The Thierrys, puzzled and pained by François's behaviour, anxious and worried about what will become of him, ultimately visit the director to get some reassurance about his situation; in the final sequence of the film they will receive his letter. Yet the longest sequence of this last section is devoted to Madame Thierry's 'monologue,' which forms a pendant to her husband's earlier very moving account of his experiences during the Occupation. These are important moments (each sequence lasts more than three minutes) where each of these 'characters' was responsible for an extended amount of dialogue and had to carry the film alone. It is in these moments (and in Mémère's earlier account of how she and Pépère decided to take in foster children) that Pialat comes closest to his ideal of filming like Lumière, turning reality into performance.

Monsieur Thierry was in fact telling his own story, and he was apparently able to overcome his nervousness at having to speak at length in front of the camera by focusing his attention on François and the family photographs he shows François as he speaks. He studiously avoids looking at the camera until after the cut that marks the end of his account of his escape from the Germans. His self-effacement in front of the camera becomes a formal corroboration of his hesitant and matter of fact – equally self-effacing – account of both the heroism and the sacrifices that marked his life during the war and the Occupation.

Madame Thierry, however, was obliged, not only to face the camera, but to project herself as a character into a fictional situation. The scene bears comparison with the scene in *Les 400 Cents Coups* where Antoine Doinel is interviewed by the psychiatrist. Both actors are filmed frontally in shallow depth of field as they attempt to respond in character. Antoine's greater poise contrasts with Madame Thierry's discomfort at being in the spotlight, even though her husband provides moral support. However, Madame Thierry's evident goodwill and nervousness enrich her character. Paradoxically, her hesitations, false starts and self-corrections contribute to her character's believability. Pialat preserves the integrity of her performance, including a moment in which, apparently intimidated by the situation, she loses her grip on the story and gropes for the name of Raoul. As it continues to elude her, she exclaims 'Ça y est ! C'est mal parti!' ('That's it! We're off to a bad start!'). Her exclamation functions on two levels, as a reflection on the reality of the filming, and on the fictional circumstances in which she attempts to convey the contradictory emotions she feels about a child who adored her mother, yet did not hesitate to steal from her granddaughter's piggybank.

François's frequent displacement from both the pictorial and narrative centre of the film, culminating in his disappearance from the story well before the final sequence (in which he is only represented by his letter) might be dismissed as concrete proof of Pialat's shifting interests during the filming. Pialat admitted that the older couple reminded him of his grandparents and that he ultimately found them far more interesting than the boy (Pialat 1974: 3). Yet he makes this displacement serve the aesthetic unity of the work, where it provides the formal counterpart to François's marginalisation and failure to find a place in a family.

The conclusion of the film connects with the opening credits in its broader focus on the family as a social unit, and the balance it establishes between children and adults. By contrast, Truffaut's film replaces the family with the friendship between Antoine and René, while the famous Guignol sequence plunges the viewer into a universe of children whose tenderness and open affection for one another represent an implicit reproach to the adults of the film. In *Les 400 Coups* the bourgeois world is corrupt, and the family, no less than the school and the justice system, fail Antoine. He escapes from the imprisoning world of adults, but remains alone in the final freeze frame. Pialat's film ends with the hope (however fragile) of the child's social reintegration into the family, which remains, for better or for worse, a crucial link between the individual and society.

If both films represent a backward look at childhood, Truffaut will rapidly move on – with *Tirez sur le pianiste, Jules et Jim* and *Antoine et Colette* – to take up the theme of the couple, a particular predilection of the *Nouvelle Vague*. Yet Pialat continually returned to the family, and the themes and concerns that characterise *L'Enfance nue* reappear in different contexts over the course of his career.

References

Bergala, Alain (1998), 'Techniques de la Nouvelle Vague', *Cahiers du cinéma: La Nouvelle Vague*, no. hors série.

Chevrie, Marc (1992), 'Pialat et la Nouvelle Vague' in *Maurice Pialat, l'enfant sauvage* Torino, Museo Nationale del cinema.

De Baecque, Antoine (1998), *La Nouvelle Vague: portrait d'une jeunesse*, Paris, Flammarion.

Frodon, Michel (1995), *L'Age moderne du cinéma français: de la Nouvelle Vague à nos jours*, Paris, Flammarion.

Holmes, Diana and Robert Ingram (1998), *François Truffaut*, Manchester/ New York, Manchester University Press.

Jeancolas, Jean-Pierre (1979), *Le Cinéma des Français: La Ve République*, Paris, Stock.

Magny, Joël (1992), *Maurice Pialat*, Paris, Cahiers du cinéma.

Marie, Michel (1997), *La Nouvelle Vague: une école artistique*, Paris, Nathan.

Pialat, Maurice (1974), 'Trois Rencontres avec Maurice Pialat', *Positif*, no. 159.

Pialat, Maurice (1979), 'Entretien', *Cahiers du cinéma*, no. 304.

Pialat, Maurice (1979b), 'Entretien', *Cinéma 72*, no. 250.

Pialat, Maurice (1980), 'Entretien', *Cinématographe*, no. 57.

Pialat, Maurice (1985), 'Les Rayures du zèbre: entretien', *Cahiers du cinéma*, no. 135.

Pialat, Maurice (1987), 'La Ligne droite: entretien avec Maurice Pialat', *Cahiers du cinéma*, no. 399.

Pialat, Maurice (2000), 'Entretien: sur la colère', *Cahiers du cinéma*, no. 550.

Prédal, René (1996), *50 ans de cinéma français*, Paris, Nathan.

Truffaut, François (1988), *Le Cinéma selon François Truffaut* (textes réunis par Anne Gillain), Paris, Flammarion.

Turk, Edward Baron (1989), *Child of Paradise: Marcel Carné and the Golden Age of French Cinema*, Cambridge and London, Harvard University Press.

1 Maurice Pialat during
the filming of *Van Gogh*.
© Photograph Luc Roux
(Coll. Bibliothèque du
film)

2 *L'Enfance nue*, 1968. (Coll. *Cahiers du cinéma*)

3 *Nous ne viellirons pas ensemble*, 1972. © Photograph Bernard Prim (Coll. Bibliothèque du film)

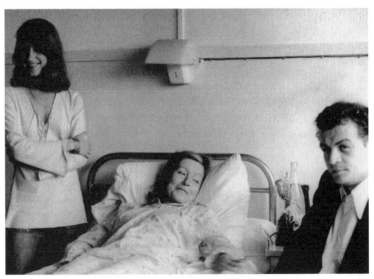

4 *La Gueule ouverte*, 1974. (Coll. *Cahiers du cinéma*/D. Rabourdin)

5 *Passe ton bac d'abord*, 1979. (Coll. *Cahiers du cinéma*)

6 *Loulou*, © Production Gaumont, 1980. (Coll. Bibliothèque du film)

7 *A nos amours*, © Production Gaumont, 1983

8 *Police*, © Production Gaumont, 1985

9 *Sous le soleil de Satan*, © Production Gaumont, 1987

10 *Van Gogh*, 1991. (Coll. Bibliothèque du film)

11 On the set of *Le Garçu*, 1995. Photograph: Marie Laure de Decker (Coll. Bibliothèque du film)

12 Maurice Pialat in *A nos amours*, © Production Gaumont, 1983

3

A family of works

One of the most striking features of Pialat's cinema is its formal and thematic coherence. Although his films treat subjects as diverse as the problem of adoption and the tragic death of a legendary painter, the autobiographical substratum of his work emerges in a number of 'primal scenarios' (the abandonment or rejection of a child, a brother or a brother-in-law's betrayal, the death of a parent, the failure of a love relationship between an older man and a much younger woman) which are reinterpreted and replayed from film to film. However, the fundamental unity of his work – and its greater artistic resonance – comes from the fact that this disguised or transposed autobiographical project takes on greater social, cultural and historical dimensions through Pialat's interest in 'the family'.

In the broadest sense, all of Pialat's films are about the family, whether this involves the interactions of parents and children (as in *L'Enfance nue, Passe ton bac d'abord, La Gueule ouverte* and *A nos amours*) or the couple whose problematic relationship will preclude their becoming a family and having a child (as in *Nous ne vieillirons ensemble, Loulou* and *Police*), or the solitary figure who will never find a place in a family – even the larger family of a community of faith – and whose isolation will be a source of much suffering (*Sous le soleil de Satan* and *Van Gogh*). Only in his final film, *Le Garçu*, does Pialat envision a couple who have conceived a child, but even here the family unit is broken and the child will have two fathers – his biological father and his mother's new partner – who compete for his affections.

A whole constellation of issues emerges from Pialat's preoccupation with the family: issues of community and national identity, generational conflict (and its historical counterpart: tradition versus change), work and money, sexuality and sexual politics, and paternity. This gives his films a political dimension that is all the more subtle for remaining implicit in the interactions of individual characters, even though the ambiguities of these interactions occasionally led viewers to accuse Pialat of anti-Semitism, racism and misogyny. Moreover, Pialat's willingness to sign a petition in favour of Valéry Giscard d'Estaing at the time of the 1974 elections alienated many in the film community and gave him, for a time at least, the reputation of a right-wing filmmaker, despite the fact that few filmmakers treated the lives of the lower-middle and working classes so sympathetically. These ambiguities remain part of Pialat's contradictions, but in the final analysis, as he himself suggested to an interviewer: 'il faut regarder les films que je fais' (Pialat 1979: 69) ('you have to look at the films I make').

Subsequent chapters will be devoted to readings of all his major films (except the television series *La Maison des bois*). This chapter will provide a frame for the analyses of individual films by presenting an overview of Pialat's filmic universe, beginning with what Pialat himself saw as a crucial determinant of an artist's talent: his or her country. While the initial sections will identify core values and major thematic issues in his work, the final sections of the chapter concentrate primarily on formal concerns, which are often overshadowed by the attention paid to Pialat's realism.

Pialat's France

'Je crois que ce qui caractérise avant tout le talent de quelqu'un, c'est son pays. Pas sa nationalité, son pays',[1] Pialat said in his last interview with *Cahiers du cinéma* (Pialat 2000: 64). There is an echo of Renoir in this evocation of an artistic *terroir*, as Renoir also insisted on the importance of the particular atmosphere, climate and soil that play their part in an artist's development. However, unlike Renoir, whose travels took him to India and the United States where he was plunged into different cultural worlds, or the *Nouvelle Vague*, whose cultural

1 'I believe that what characterises someone's talent above all is his or her country. Not his or her nationality, his or her country.'

references reflected their wide-ranging cinematic tastes, Pialat's work is deeply rooted in French culture. Critics considered him one of the rare filmmakers to portray the reality of small-town and rural France, *la France profonde*. Although for Joël Magny, this is to be taken more in the sense of a group of characters to whom Pialat offers equal opportunities in his narratives, 'par opposition à une France hiérarchisée dont le reste du cinéma français n'offre le plus souvent que le haut de la pyramide (moyenne et grande bourgeoisie)'[2] (Magny 1992: 52).

Nonetheless, Pialat's depiction of life in provincial towns, the northern mining towns that figure in *L'Enfance nue* and *Passe ton bac d'abord* or the Auvergne of *La Gueule ouverte* and *Le Garçu*, had such authenticity that reviewers and critics wrongly assumed that it was based on personal experience. Pialat's attraction to these regions can be traced to his family origins: *une ascendance picarde* on his mother's side; his father's native Auvergne – but despite his admiration for Pagnol, Pialat never imagined being a regional artist. In fact, *Le Garçu*, his last film, presents most poignantly the loss of the provincial roots that might have given his main character, Gérard, a sense of place or identity.

Pialat's childhood and adolescence were indelibly marked by his family's move from Auvergne to the Parisian suburbs, so that his sense of place was bound up with a feeling of loss and displacement. His uprooting finds an echo in his characters' many sudden departures, some having the wrenching finality of rejection (François in *L'Enfance nue*, gazing mutely out the car window as he is driven away from his first foster family; Catherine's unexpected disappearance in *Nous ne vieillirons pas ensemble*; Donissan's 'exile' to the Trappist monastery in *Sous le soleil de Satan*) – others offering the hope of escape (Philippe and Bernard's heading to Paris at the end of *Passe ton bac d'abord*, Suzanne's trip to San Diego in the final sequence of *A nos amours*, Noria's flight at the end of *Police*). Pialat also creates a sense of displacement by the fragmented way he treats geographic space in his films. He frequently dispenses with exterior and establishing shots, and as Philippe Carcassonne notes, generally excludes 'une approche centrale, "essentielle", du lieu'[3] that would situate events for the

2 'by contrast to a hierarchical France of which the rest of French cinema most frequently offers only the top of the pyramid (middle and upper-middle classes)'.

3 'a central "essentialist" approach to location'.

viewer (Carcassonne 1980: 14). The rich sense of place conveyed by Pialat's films emanates instead from his characters, the fine detail of their existence, the spaces in which they interact, whether this be Mémé's kitchen in *L'Enfance nue*, Catherine's grandmother's house in *Nous ne vieillirons pas ensemble*, or, tellingly, the restaurant in which Gérard makes himself at home in *Le Garçu*.

Consequently Pialat's representation of *la France profonde* has less to do with a place or a mythic image of rural France, the village set close to its church and framed by its fields, than with the representation of a particular class, lower-middle-class or working-class France – the people who 'take the Métro'. Philippe Carcassonne argued that Pialat was the first filmmaker to challenge the dominant hierarchical cultural model that associated complex emotional and moral feelings with a more educated upper class. 'Grâce à lui, les ouvriers, les retraités, les commerçants ... les petits bourgeois qui composent l'essentiel de son univers se découvrent et nous découvrent une complexité affective jusque là réservée à quelque élite moderne occupée au détail complaisant de ses malaises'[4] (Carcassonne 1980: 14). Not that bourgeois pretensions or malaise are absent from Pialat's films, but they take the form of the frequently odious and inevitably patronising bourgeois 'other' (the Parisian photographers in *Passe ton bac d'abord*, Nelly's brother – and to a lesser degree her husband – in *Loulou*, 'the brother-in-law' in *A nos amours*, Dr Gachet in *Van Gogh*, and arguably even the Bishop in *Sous le soleil de Satan*).

Pialat's France is also primarily the France of the 1970s and 1980s – from Pompidou through to Giscard d'Estaing to Mitterrand – the period during which eight of his films were made and the period in which they were set. The 'crise' – or economic slump – that dominates this period, putting an end to post-war economic expansion, surfaces most clearly in *Passe ton bac d'abord* (1979), whose protagonists see no future for themselves even if they pass their exams; in *Loulou* (1980) where only one of the working-class men has a job and the main character turns more readily to theft or non-violent crime; and to a lesser extent in the more stereotypical *Police* (1985) where the increasing fragmentation of French society and the difficulties of

---

4 'Thanks to him, the workers, the retired persons, the shopkeepers ... the petty bourgeois who made up the bulk of his universe, discovered in themselves and revealed to us the emotional complexity that up to that point had been reserved for some modern elite self-indulgently analysing its malaises.'

assimilating immigrant populations with different cultural norms are filtered through the genre of the *polar*.

However, the France of the 1970s and 1980s coexists in Pialat's films with an older France – the Third Republic of Bernanos's *Sous le soleil de Satan*, the France of Pialat's grandparents; or France during the war and the Occupation, the France of Pialat's parents' maturity – that is most frequently embodied in the parents and grandparents of his main characters. Although in *Loulou*, Nelly's husband will regret the changing landscape of their neighbourhood, pointing out that the butcher shop, grocery store and corner bakery have all disappeared, replaced by trendy restaurants and antique dealers. By the mid-1980s the multiplication of different life styles coupled with a gradual erosion in shared values led a popular sociological reference to observe that 'il y a de moins en moins de racines, de traditions, de mythes du passé qui mobilisent tous les Français dans une même aventure culturelle'[5] (Mermet 1985: 410). Pialat's work reflects this, capturing gradual changes in the rhythm and patterns of family life over several generations in a decade of films.

Families and generational conflict

Rarely primary characters, parents and grandparents remain on the fringes of *Nous ne vieillirons pas ensemble*, *Passe ton bac d'abord* and *A nos amours*, but provide a form of narrative depth by connecting the family to tradition and history. In *L'Enfance nue* (completed in 1969), this is doubly reinforced because the 'parents', the Thierrys, are already grandparents themselves when they take in François, their second foster child, and the family circle includes Madame Thierry's very elderly mother, Mémère-la-vieille. The closeness of the generations, who share a single space, is represented not only by Monsieur Thierry's passing on the story of the family's heroism and hardships during the Occupation to François, but also (primarily) through François's love for Mémère-la vieille. The sequence in which they sing traditional songs, 'Gentil Coquelicot' and 'Mon père m'a donné un mari', underscores their affection and their shared heritage. The film

5 'there are fewer and fewer roots, traditions, myths about the past which involve all of the French in a single cultural experience'.

again alludes to this shared culture during a wedding reception where the young bride sings a song of her parents' generation, Fréhel's 'La Java bleue' from the late 1930s. Pialat will return to such songs, a shared cultural legacy, in *Passe ton bac d'abord* where, in what is perhaps a reminiscence of Renoir, Elisabeth's father's sings 'Frou-frou' at another wedding reception. *Van Gogh* features performances of 'Le Temps des cerises' and 'La Butte rouge', while in *Le Garçu* the songs are nursery songs and games taught to young children.

In *Nous ne vieillirons pas ensemble*, Catherine's grandmother links the family to its history and traditions. Yet the film suggests the fading of the grandparents' importance to the family, as the grand-mother complains of her isolation in the large house she bought to accommodate visits from her children and grandchildren during vacations. Her grandchildren no longer visit her regularly and her son never comes to see her, preferring to drive the family to the Riviera. She sees no progress in his acquisition of a car, claiming the train is cheaper – and she remains attached to a rural past through her kitchen garden. Although she shakes her head over her grand-daughter's lack of interest in housework and looks askance at her taste in clothing, the grandmother attempts to remain involved in the life of the family, even though her son warns her that she will die 'la gueule ouverte'.[6]

Pialat's next three films focus on a nuclear family in which grand-parents no longer play a role. Moreover, *La Gueule ouverte* (1974), *Passe ton bac d'abord* (1979) and *A nos amours* (1983), arguably Pialat's richest and most powerful films, are all centred on a crucial moment when the family unit is divided and will ultimately break apart. This is the result of the mother's death in *La Gueule ouverte* and the loss of the father in *A nos amours*, while *Passe ton bac d'abord* follows a group of students in their final year of school as they begin to move out into the world. While *La Gueule ouverte* remains within the narrow frame of two couples, the ageing parents and their son and his wife, even in *Passe ton bac d'abord* and *A nos amours*, which involve larger family groupings, the sense of a united multi-generational family has clearly lost any real currency. When Bernard and Patrick fantasise about escaping the dead-end life they envision in Lens (in *Passe ton bac*

6 'with her mouth open'. [The remark intended to underscore the fact that no one will care.]

d'abord), they consider visiting Patrick's (supposedly rich) aunt who lives in Paris, but Patrick has not seen her for nine years. Similarly the family reception that forms the penultimate sequence in *A nos amours* does not include aunts, uncles or grandparents, just immediate family and employees of the family business.

Family business

Money is as important a theme in Pialat's films as it is in Balzac's novels, and the fear that she could not afford a child ultimately leads Nelly to have an abortion in *Loulou*. Yet at the same time Pialat rarely gives much insight into the working lives of his families. Only brief glimpses are provided into the community of miners that frames the action in *L'Enfance nue* and *Passe ton bac d'abord*; this is equally true of the more artisanal work of the furrier in *A nos amours*. The primary exception is *Police*, where the nature of police work is an integral part of the subject. Yet the most common situation in Pialat's films is that the working community forms a family, like that of the miners or the police, or that 'work' means the 'family' business. The emphasis on the family business also reflects an older France, that of Pialat's parents, and their parents, in which the father is both the head of the family and the *patron* (boss) who runs the small shop or artisanal enterprise that supports the family and is a pillar of the community. Pialat himself observed that his view of the family was shaped primarily by this nineteenth-century model, observing to an interviewer: 'Vous connaissez les livres de l'historien Ariès sur l'éducation et la famille qui dit que cette formule familale, allant de pair avec le nationalisme et le paternalisme, et qui m'a impregné, a disparu en 1940. J'étais en plein potage'[7] (Pialat 1980: 5).

It is one measure of the conservative sexual politics of Pialat's films that few of the women in his films have jobs of any significance outside the family in a period during which the number of women working outside the home was steadily increasing. The mothers: Betty in *A nos amours* and Monique in *La Gueule ouverte*, worked in the family business, while Loulou's mother (the father is absent,

7 'You know the books by the historian Ariès on education and the family, which say that this conception of the family, associated with nationalism and paternalism, which I absorbed, disappeared in 1940. I was right in the middle of it.'

perhaps deceased) works as a cleaning lady. Catherine in *Nous ne vieillirons pas ensemble* works, desultorily, at secretarial jobs while dreaming of a career in modelling, but she is primarily marking time until she marries. The younger generation of working-class women in *Passe ton bac d'abord* is either unemployed or, like the newly married Agnès, in unskilled jobs – she is a cashier in a *grande surface*. Even Nelly in *Loulou*, a woman of the 1980s, a cultivated bourgeoise – the one woman in the film who supports her male partner – works (until he fires her) for her former husband.

Yet in *La Gueule ouverte*, the formal parallel between the dying mother, Monique, and her daughter-in-law Nathalie throws into relief the greater changes in the family and in women's lives over a generation. Not considered particularly intelligent, Monique was not encouraged to finish her schooling, and her husband belittled her lack of education. While she worked to help to make ends meet, she tolerated, but bitterly resented, his philandering and frequent escapes to local bars. By contrast, Nathalie is neither dependent nor submissive and works outside the family, although her work does not appear to have the status of a 'career'. No children tie her to her husband and she is quick to reproach him for his failings. As though she were attempting to reject her role as the younger counterpart of her mother-in-law, Nathalie is also the one most frequently absent from the space of the family drama, remaining, literally, out of the picture because of her job. If she does resemble her mother-in-law, it is in her ambivalence towards her marriage and her resentment towards her husband and his family. This might plausibly lead to divorce, as the number of divorces increased significantly from just over 20 million in 1925 (when Pialat was born) to just over 50 million by 1975, the year after the film was made (Mermet 1985: 81).

However, most of the daughters in Pialat's films: Elisabeth and Agnès in *Passe ton bac d'abord*, Catherine in *Nous ne vieillirons pas ensemble*, even Nelly in *Loulou*, marry (whether out of choice or for lack of choices) rather than striking out on their own. Suzanne, in *A nos amours*, will marry, then (like her father) abandon her partner; but only Noria, typed as a *femme fatale* in *Police*, will choose her freedom. The universe of Pialat's work is shaped by the contradiction between the persistence of a conservative, patriarchal vision of the family and the effects of a changing economic and social climate. Yet this gives his films an added dimension of realism precisely because they reflect

the very real lag between changing attitudes and actual social change
(Powrie 1997: 10).

Family, cruelty and the human condition

For Pialat, as for Renoir, meals have an important function in the
representation of the social universe, providing insight into the
strength of the community or family unit and the stresses that
undermine it. Meals are such a repeated motif in Pialat's films that an
exhaustive list would be overwhelming, but of the innumerable meals,
or social occasions involving meals, only the wedding reception in
L'Enfance nue is without significant underlying tensions. Worse still,
in the case of *Passe ton bac d'abord*, *Loulou* and *A nos amours*, moments
that might have been an apotheosis of social harmony lead instead to
violence and the flight or expulsion of a member of the community.

This reflects the fact that what Pialat's families can offer of love,
understanding, acceptance, recognition and support does not always
come in time, or at the right time, and Pialat's characters often fail
each other. The pain of this failure is compounded because in many
cases the characters perversely act against their own best interests,
alienating the very people they love most and whose love and support
they most need. Joël Magny sees in this a 'cruelty' that he identifies as
the dominant element of Pialat's universe, a recurring formal figure
and a major theme (Magny 1992: 41). Jean Narboni puts a slightly
different slant on it, describing Pialat's universe as one of 'personnes
déplacées' (displaced persons), characters who fail to fit in and
consequently can never be at home, never entirely comfortable in
their own skin (Narboni 1979: 5). Pialat's particular dramaturgy: his
avoidance of 'psychology'; his decision to begin his narratives just as
the social system – which had previously been in some precarious
equilibrium – begins to break down, deprives the viewer of insight
into the causes, immediate or long term, that led to the breakdown,
intensifying the sense that the patriarchal family, as a centre and a
central value, cannot hold, but that there is nothing to replace it.

Narboni's characterisation of Pialat's world, in which 'le mal est
fait' (the evil deed is done, something irrevocable has happened) long
before the viewer enters the picture, suggests a quasi-theological
dimension to Pialat's universe that assimilates both the individual

and the family's failure to a kind of original sin. If the filmmaker would hardly have sanctioned such a view, it is nonetheless true that a deep current of sadness, not entirely distinguishable from profound pessimism, about the nature of the human community and the human condition runs through Pialat's work. It surfaces clearly in Mangin's rephrasing of Chardonne in *Police*, 'le fond de tout est horrible' ('at bottom everything is horrible') and in Pialat's citing Van Gogh's remark: 'la tristesse durera toujours' ('the sadness will last forever') in *A nos amours*. Pialat's struggle against this fundamental pessimism emerges most clearly in *Police* where his alter ego Mangin asserts both the importance of work well done and the value of human life. Mangin's toast to the birth of a child at the end of *Police* provides a counterpart to Chardonne and reaffirms the important symbolic place of the child in Pialat's films. A couple's desire for a child, their decision to have a child (or to end a pregnancy), the attention given a child, the possibilities offered a child all become a measure of the family and the society in which the child must find a place.

The couple

Pialat once asserted that 'il n'y aurait pas d'histoires si on se reproduisait comme des escargots. Il n'y aurait pas de nations, pas de sociétés, pas de guerre'[8] (Pialat 1984: 17). Three films: *Nous ne vieillirons pas ensemble*, *Loulou* and *Police* focus on this fundamental social unit, the couple, portraying both the centripetal forces – desire, loneliness and fear among them – that draw two individuals together, and the competing centrifugal forces – disappointments and betrayals both great and small – that inevitably pull them apart. 'Inevitably' can be the only appropriate word because there are no happy endings for Pialat's love stories, and if children are not wholly absent from these films they are always someone else's. Of the three films about couples, only *Loulou* concludes with the couple still together, although their union is as fragile as it is unstable. The film's final frame shows Nelly staggering under the weight of the drunken Loulou as they lurch off uncertainly into the night. Pialat's films about couples are

8 'there would be no problems [but also no stories] if we reproduced like snails. There would be no nations, no societies, no war'.

intensely personal, intensely physical, both vulgar and violent. Certainly the male partners demonstrate that they are fully capable of physical aggression – even if in *Nous ne vieillirons pas ensemble* the couples' verbal assaults on each other ultimately do equal damage to their relationship. Yet the films convey the depth and intensity of the couples' relationships most powerfully through the physical presence of the actors who embody emotions which their characters are unable to articulate: Catherine's fearful shrinking away from Jean in *Nous ne vieillirons pas ensemble*; Nelly and Loulou entwined together in bed, the epitome of sexual satisfaction; Mangin, walking away from the final kiss Noria offers him in *Police*.

'J'ai filmé des histoires de couples particulièrement ... je ne dirai pas sordides, parce que les histoires de couples *sont* sordides', Pialat admitted, 'je les ai peut-être réalisées de manière un peu sordide, mais c'est vrai que ça intéresse, c'est universel'9 (Pialat 1984: 17). If Pialat tended to dismiss the subject as both sordid and banal, his interest in the couple links his work thematically with that of the New Wave. However, Pialat's films about couples also represent the intersection of the personal and the social in ways that differentiate them from the New Wave's treatment of the same subject. Pialat's couples, for all the intensity of the personal and sexual dimension of their relationship, never fully sever their ties with the larger social universe symbolised by the family. Certainly the alienation and social marginality of Michel in Godard's *A bout de souffle*; his 'Pierrot' in *Pierrot le fou*, or Truffaut's Charlie in *Tirez sur le pianiste*, find parallels in Loulou, or Mangin – even Jean in *Nous ne vieillirons pas ensemble* is marginalised by his difficult personality and his lack of professional success. Yet where Godard intensifies his couples' marginality by pairing Michel or Pierrot with a woman who is foreign, a Jean Seberg or Anna Karina, and Truffaut's Charlie retreats behind his piano after losing his wife and then his new love, Pialat's couples remain enmeshed in a larger network of relationships. The parents, siblings and other relatives or associates of Pialat's couples move in and out of the frame, their approval, or more frequently disapproval, of the couple's relationship complicating both the relationship and the story.

9 'I've filmed stories about couples particularly ... I won't say sordid, because stories about couples *are* sordid, but perhaps I made them in a way that was slightly sordid, but it's true that they are interesting, they're universal.'

Sex, triangles and sexual politics

The centrality of masculine desire to Pialat's cinema parallels the central role accorded to the father, and coincides with the author/director's vision, even when it is identified with that of a central female character, as in the case of Suzanne in *A nos amours*. Sex is important to the men in Pialat's films, but it is neither coloured by eroticism nor hedged around with courtly gestures. It is instinctive, and powerfully physical, like Loulou's attraction to Nelly, and Pialat's films are full of *dragueurs* (womanisers) who can be crudely appraising of a woman's physical charms. Yet Pialat's men are also very vulnerable despite their machismo and the virile masculine image they project. Apparently misogynist, even abusive, they are also profoundly attached to the women they denigrate or dismiss, women who are themselves capable of sharp remarks that wound deeply.

However, sex is no less important to Pialat's women than his men. Even though Catherine tells Jean in *Nous ne vieillirons pas ensemble* that they have no future as a couple, she attempts to negotiate the possibility that they will continue to make love. For Suzanne in *A nos amours*, making love is both a pleasure and an escape. 'On oublie tout, tu ne trouves pas' ('You forget everything, don't you think'), she tells one of her many lovers. Nelly will leave her bourgois husband for Loulou, who 'never stops', while in *Le Garçu* Cathy will be seized with a sudden amorous urge in a parking garage. Elisabeth in *Passe ton bac d'abord* has slept with all of the young men in her group, and even the prim bourgeoise, Frédérique, who meets the friends camping on the beach, will end up propositioning Bernard, the group's Lothario. This might be considered a masculine director's projection onto his female characters, however, it is also true that Pialat's characters remain unsatisfied by sex, looking for something more, something that the proprietor of the café in *Passe ton bac d'abord* reduces to a 'little tenderness'. The disillusioned adolescent Patrick astonishes Elisabeth's older sister in *Passe ton bac d'abord* by telling her that he is tired of sex, while the relationship between Jean and Catherine founders despite their sexual compatibility. In *A nos amours*, Suzanne remains obsessively attached to Luc, the one boy with whom she never actually had a sexual relationship. Even Loulou, a virile, tough character, fears that women are attracted to him only for the sexual pleasure he provides, and the possibility of a child with

Nelly clearly offers him a future, which until then he had never envisioned.

One of the complications of the couples' relationships is the degree to which it is triangulated by the presence of an ex-wife or an ex-husband who remains in the picture, if in the background, becoming a rival for the new partner; or by a parent who serves as a model, shaping the son or daughter's desires and expectations. This goes all the way back to the father, Roger Bastide, in *La Gueule ouverte*, whose own father (long dead) had such strong views on class that Roger was driven into an unsatisfying marriage. In *Nous ne vieillirons pas ensemble* Jean continues to live with his wife, Françoise, despite his six-year liaison with Catherine. André hovers in the background, hoping to convince Nelly to return in *Loulou*; and in *A nos amours* Suzanne measures all of her lovers against her father, wondering if he would approve of them. In the case of Philippe, Elisabeth's boyfriend in *Passe ton bac d'abord*, who grew up in an orphanage, Elisabeth's family is part of her attraction. Although the fact that Elisabeth's parents readily welcome him into the family subsequently leads Elisabeth to view her mother as a potential rival. Through such triangulations the family intervenes in the life of the couple, sometimes even when the partners are well into middle age.

A crisis of masculinity and the *cinéma de papa*

In the case of three films of the 1980s, *Loulou*, *A nos amours* and *Police*, these triangulations also focus attention on pairs of male characters (one feminised by the association) who function as doubles and/or rivals and whose relationships have a homoerotic charge only partly dissipated by the female character who completes the triangle. Loulou is paired with Nelly's ex-husband André in *Loulou*; in *A nos amours* Michel, the son, is played off against the father, Roger, in their relationship with the mother, Betty, and their quasi-incestuous love for Suzanne. In *Police*, Mangin and Lambert are linked by their sexual relationships with the prostitute Lydie and with Noria. This masculine pairing takes another form in Pialat's adaptation of *Sous le soleil de Satan*, where the main character, the priest Donissan (Depardieu) is guided into self-sacrificing sainthood by his mentor and spiritual director, the Dean Menou-Segrais (Pialat). Depardieu is feminised both as an actor and a character by his acquiescence to Menou-Segrais/Pialat's 'authorial' direction. The film underlines the importance of Pialat's character in this regard by having him reappear at the film's conclusion to put, literally, the final touch to his creation. The pairing of masculine characters continues in Pialat's films of the 1990s: *Van Gogh*, where Vincent and Théo are brother rivals, and *Le Garçu* where the two 'fathers' compete for the son's affection – although in both cases the homoerotic charge is defused by a compensatory multiplication of feminine figures.

Dominique Besnehard, who worked with Pialat on casting several films before taking on the role of the son in *A nos amours*, implied that this feminisation was inevitably the fate of Pialat's male stars, who were stand-ins for the director, indirectly competing with him by assuming his role in the narrative. Besnehard admitted that he remained a little angry with Pialat for having displaced him as the primary masculine role in the *A nos amours* (Besnehard 2003: 39) – noting in another interview: 'on est dévirilisé chez Maurice Pialat obligatoirement' (Pialat 1984: 156) ('one is inevitably feminised by working with Maurice Pialat'). This obligatory feminisation is reflected in the high degree of tension between Pialat and most of his masculine stars: Jean Yanne, Philippe Léotard, and at least initially on *Loulou*, Gérard Depardieu. However, Depardieu's powerful combination of a traditional image of 'aggressive French machismo' (in films from *Les Valseuses* to *Cyrano de Bergerac*) with a certain sexual ambiguity (Vincendeau 2000: 228–9) also makes him an ideal double for the director. Depardieu's status as the dominant actor in Pialat's films of the 1980s (three out of four films) also coincides with what Phil Powrie identified as a 'crisis of masculinity' in French film beginning with 'the advent of feminism' in the 1970s and fuelled by the impact of increasing numbers of working women on lifestyles and sex roles (Powrie 1997: 8–9).

The feminisation of Pialat's male characters in his 1980s films emerges most clearly in their failure to create a family and become fathers, highlighting the importance of paternity in his work. The fact that Pialat's central male characters in the 1970s and 1980s are 'sons' also connects his work with that of the New Wave and the revolt of the Young Turks against the *cinéma de papa*. Yet Pialat's cinema never deliberately seeks to break completely with the older tradition the fathers represent. Instead, the frequent presence or evocation of fathers in these films emphasises a continuity that is summed up in references to the father as 'le garçu': the *auvergnat* patois designating the 'father' as 'his father's son'. Pialat's sons may not get along with their fathers, like Bernard in *Passe ton bac d'abord*, but they consider that it is at least partly their fault. Yet internal family stresses and generational differences rooted in social and economic change inevitably mean that the sons do not wish to follow in their fathers' footsteps. The sons do not openly rebel, but have difficulty finding their place, torn between their provincial roots and the break with the past that will be necessary to live their own lives. Their hesitations are reflected in the back-and-forth movement between Paris and the provinces that marks many of Pialat's films. The sons' ambivalence also has repercussions for the couple because the male characters have a tendency to prolong their status as sons by turning their wives into mother substitutes and/or establishing relationships with much younger women who might otherwise be the age of their daughters.

This father–son ambivalence emerges fully in *A nos amours* where Pialat himself plays the role of a father who – after walking out on his wife and children – returns to reassert his paternal authority during a family reception celebrating his son's growing reputation as a writer. He castigates the son, telling him that he has become so enamoured of his own success that he has forgotten 'where he came from', yet vehemently defends his son's art against corrupting moneyed interests represented by the son's own brother-in-law.

The tension between generations, the profound ambivalence, the intense pain, love and hate generated by family bonds (or the lack of them) that is at the heart of Pialat's cinema is then also replayed in Pialat's relationship with the *Nouvelle Vague*. His sentimental attachment to the *tradition de qualité* or *cinéma de papa*, despite his divergence from the aesthetic norms that characterised it, is the exact counterpart of his stubborn rejection of the *Nouvelle Vague* and his unwillingness to admit any family resemblance between his films and the ideals of the Young Turks.

Formal ambivalence

Pialat's ambivalence towards the *Nouvelle Vague* also takes the form of a certain resistance to the label 'realist' filmmaker. 'Le réalisme, au fond, je n'y crois pas', he told interviewers at *Positif*, 'On fait du réalisme ou du naturalisme faute de moyens. La même scène tournée avec des moyens devient autre chose'[10] (Pialat 1984: 7). His belief that 'realist' films – at least in the wake of the *Nouvelle Vague* – were condemned to small budgets certainly contributed to this resistance. However, Pialat was more strongly influenced by his admiration for the Lumière brothers than by the critics at *Cahiers du cinéma*, and his realism stems primarily from a desire to capture or recreate real events in images. He confessed that his attachment to anecdotal reality was so strong he sometimes found it paralysing. Not only did it hamper him when he tried to graft fictional events onto real ones when working on a scenario, but, as he told Catherine Breillat, he found it impossible to film in a grey room with the bed in the middle if he knew that in the real story the room was blue and the bed was against the wall (Breillat 1992: 227). This desire for authenticity extended to formal and technical concerns: his choice of focal lengths approximating human vision (and an avoidance of extreme close-ups and panoramic views) and his efforts to preserve the integrity of a scene by filming it in a single long take – or '*plan-séquence*'. He usually adhered to a strictly chronological presentation of events that excluded even such an established narrative convention as parallel editing. There is only one flashback in all of his ten films (at the end of *Nous ne vieillirons pas ensemble*) – not counting the brief appearance of Mouchette's ghost in *Sous le Soleil de Satan*. Pialat was also adamant about the importance of authentic sound, even though he sometimes resorted to dubbing and non-synchronous sound to obtain greater clarity in dialogues. He shied away from extra-diagetic music in his early work, and particularly regretted its inclusion in *A nos amours* where Suzanne sits alone in the rain at a bus stop, claiming that he should have used the low rumble of thunder from the storm instead. Yet despite his fixation on authenticity, his work frequently undermines realist conventions to create effects of a different order.

10 'Basically, I don't believe in realism [...] You are realist or naturalist because you lack the means to do otherwise. The same scene shot with more money becomes something else.'

Plan-séquences **versus montage**

'Je pars de faits banaux et … c'est plus fort que moi – je vais jusqu'au bout' (Pialat 1980: 8) ('I start with banal facts, and … I can't help myself, I go as far as possible'). One of Pialat's most frequent laments when he completed a film was that 'on aurait pu aller beaucoup plus loin' – he could 'have gone much farther': developed and refined his subject; improved on his first efforts (Pialat 1979: 61). His shifts in direction or focus in the course of filming created difficulties as early as the 1970s: 'J'ai un gros travail de montage parce que je ne découpe pas', he told an interviewer. 'Il m'arrive souvent d'être en bout de séquences et de ne pas savoir comment passer à la suivante parce que je n'ai pas prévu ou même voulu tourner le plan de rien du tout qui m'aurait permis de passer d'une chose à l'autre'[11] (Pialat 1974: 106). Yet the overwhelming importance Pialat attributed to the actors' presence in front of the camera (reflected in the weight given to the *plan-séquence* during the actual process of filming) is offset by the crucial role that increasingly devolved to editing in the construction of the filmic narrative (where cuts, gaps and breaks assume particular importance). 'Effectivement, le montage devrait n'avoir chez moi aucune importance, or, il en a beaucoup'[12] he admitted during the editing of *Nous ne vieillirons pas ensemble* (Pialat 1974: 106).

Pialat initially viewed editing as a practical necessity, more a way of patching things together than an aesthetic practice. He claimed his approach was purely pragmatic: 'Je garde tout ce que je crois bon ou tout ce qui, du moins, ne m'apparaît pas comme mauvais. Je n'hésite pas à avoir un trou; si quelque chose est trop mauvais je le fais sauter, quand bien même la compréhension en souffrirait'[13] (Pialat 1974: 10). Yet throughout his career the editing stage was a difficult moment in which the entire project seemed threatened by the necessity to establish a narrative frame that could accommodate the best material.

---

11 'I have an enormous editing job because I don't work out a shooting script … I often find myself at the end of a sequence without knowing how to move on to the next because I didn't plan ahead or didn't want to shoot the little nothing scene that would have allowed me to move from one thing to another.'

12 'In fact, editing shouldn't have any importance in my work, but it has a good deal'.

13 'I keep everything that I think is good, or at least what doesn't appear to me to be bad. I don't hesitate to leave gaps: if something is too bad I leave it out even if makes the story more difficult to understand.'

Pialat's desire to see what would happen during the filming inevitably led – as budgets permitted – to devoting more time to the process; in his later films this sometimes stretched over an exhausting thirteen or fourteen weeks. Yann Dedet, who worked with Pialat on five films, claimed he was 'un des plus gros bouffeurs de pellicule du cinéma français' (Dedet 2003: 46) ('one of the greatest devourers of filmstock in French cinema'). There were six hours of filmed material for the luncheon at Dr Gachet's in *Van Gogh*; it took two months to pare them down to five minutes of actual screen time (Dedet 2003: 45). The final stage of filmmaking then required deciding what to discard, the difficult process of elimination complicated by the need to integrate fortuitous accidents or particularly magical moments even if they were peripheral to the storyline. This inevitably put considerable pressure on the editing to hold the film together. In weighing the different narrative possibilities latent in the material, Pialat sometimes worked with a number of different editors on a single film. Yann Dedet was perhaps the most influential of these editors, shaping Pialat's tendency to cut boldly into sequences, eliminating their formal beginnings or endings, and encouraging his striking use of *faux raccords* (false matches) and abrupt cuts.

Unlike classical realist cinema, which creates the illusion of a coherent world operating according to a recognisable logic, and forges a sense of spatial and temporal continuity out of a sequence of discrete images, Pialat's films deliberately sacrifice both coherence and continuity in order to exploit the emotive value of sudden shifts, breaks or gaps. As Pialat observed to Cyril Collard after the filming of *A nos amours*:

> Tout à coup il y a des ruptures de ton, des changements de rythme, des choses qui passent qui ne sont pas si réalistes que ça. Ça donne une émotion d'un autre ordre qui vaut à mon avis largement celle qui survient dans un découpage classique.[14] (Pialat 1984: 12)

Pialat's distaste for 'little nothing' transitions and his unwillingness to waste time building scenes to a climactic moment whose causes would be clearly evident to the viewer leaves his characters

14 'Suddenly there are breaks in tone, and changes in rhythm, things that happen that aren't all that realistic. This produces an emotion of another order which in my opinion is just as valuable as the emotion elicited by more traditionally developed shooting scripts.'

with an essential opacity and unpredictability, their abrupt changes in mood; their unpredictable reactions or sudden impulsive decisions changing the rhythm or even the course of events. Nothing in *Police* explains the sudden shift between Noria's hostility and her tearfulness during her long interrogation; nothing prepares the viewer for the juxtaposition of the Sunday luncheon at Loulou's mother with Nelly's abortion in *Loulou*, or for Suzanne's announcement that she is leaving for San Diego in *A nos amours*.

The gaps and breaks call attention to what is missing, lost moments during which something has happened, if only in the mind of the characters. If this suggests a realism of another order in which the characters continue to live their own lives outside the frame of the filmic narrative, it also marks the limits of Pialat's realism. He does not convey the logic of his character's changing thoughts or motives, registering only the words and actions that are their formal consequences. Without masking the gaps in his story, he creates a narrative whole through other formal means.

Rhythms and rhymes

Vincent Amiel analyses Pialat's films as a key example of what he terms 'le montage de correspondances', a form of editing that subordinates the organic links between sequences and shots to internal 'rhythms' and 'rhymes' (Amiel 2001: 74). The rhythms in Pialat's films are inextricably bound up with his idiosyncratic treatment of time as a juxtaposition of present moments. His resistance to creating the illusion of the passage of time is particularly striking in *Sous le soleil de Satan*, where the protagonists do not age even though the events supposedly took place over more than forty years. Pialat's films function as a concatenation of different present states that can complement or stand in contradiction to one another, dilating into *plan-séquences* or contracting into a single shot. While *plan-séquences* can stretch out the present moment almost beyond endurance, the breaks between them can be black holes that swallow days or months. Pialat also makes use of shifts or sudden changes within a scene or sequence to vary the tone and with it the rhythm: the rapid acceleration of an exchange into a hysterical scene in *A nos amours*, the dog's sudden attack on a hen in *Loulou*, the moving rendition of *Le*

Temps des cerises that mutes the hilarity of the luncheon in *Van Gogh*; the quiet despair of Mouchette's suicidal gesture shattered by the crash of the priest battering down her door in *Sous le Soleil de Satan*.

These variations in tempo are also frequently associated with repeated situations, images (or even phrases such as 'elle sent bon ma sœur' in *A nos amours*) to create motifs and internal rhymes that structure the narrative: the many conversations in Jean's car in *Nous ne vieillirons pas ensemble*, or the mother's hysterical scenes in *A nos amours*; the frequent rendez-vous at Le Caron in *Passe ton bac d'abord*; the repeated interrogations in *Police*; the nocturnal scenes in *Sous le soleil de Satan* or the dance scenes in *Van Gogh* and *Loulou*. There are also more purely visual motifs: the bed in *Loulou*, or the window and the contrast of light and shadow in *Sous le soleil de Satan*. Such repetitions establish a network of parallels and mirrorings whose formal coherence offsets gaps in the sequential progression of the narrative.

Representing the invisible

Pialat's characteristic narrative fragmentation takes on particular significance in his last major films: *Sous le soleil de Satan* and *Van Gogh*. Both presented seemingly insurmountable problems for a realist filmmaker because they focused on the life and death of an extraordinary individual – saint or great artist – whose uniqueness resided in a radically different vision and experience of reality. Pialat welcomed *Sous le soleil de Satan* as a change from his habitual realism, relying more on special effects in this film than in any of his earlier work. Ultimately however, the powerful supernatural events of Bernanos's novel, like the nature of the saint's apprehension of them, remain invisible and incomprehensible to the viewer, manifesting themselves as breaks in the narrative: the sudden appearance of the horse trader, the barely perceptible gap that precedes the priest's sudden awareness of the presence of the devil, the startling shift in point of view (from a low to a high angle shot) that constitutes the false miracle. In this film the gaps and breaks not only mark the passage of time, but also an essential and unrepresentable change in the nature of reality, whose expression Pialat consigns exclusively to the work of montage (Amiel 2001: 101, 104).

The supernatural never intrudes in *Van Gogh*, but the fact that Pialat attempts to portray one of the most original (and troubled) artistic sensibilities of nineteenth-century French art almost exclusively through the commonplace events of the artist's final days suggests the difficulty of the project. Pialat focuses on the man rather than the artist, the depths of his character evoked primarily by lingering close-ups of his face. Pialat shows Van Gogh's anger and his frustration, but the nature of the artist's profound despair and the real reasons for his decision to take his life remain his own secret. The artist merely appears, already mortally wounded, then dies alone, surrounded by the bustling activity of his boardinghouse.

Amiel locates the originality of *Van Gogh* in Pialat's refusal to portray his subject with historical hindsight. Instead the film follows the ongoing present of the painter's life, making it impossible to distinguish the ultimate importance or significance of particular events. Yet it is the gap between the more or less banal, seemingly unpredictable or haphazard events of the artist's life, and the legend that shapes the viewer's perception of them that creates a new perspective on the artist (Amiel 2001: 107). Troubling and disconcerting, both *Sous le Soleil de Satan* and *Van Gogh* undercut the viewer's certainty about the nature and meaning of events as Pialat attempts to use Lumières' medium to represent what cannot be seen.

The next two chapters will examine six films, most of them autobiographical in inspiration, that focus either on the couple or the family, although the categories blur because Pialat's couples are never without family connections. These six films: *Nous ne vieillirons pas ensemble*, *La Gueule ouverte*, *Passe ton bac d'abord*, *Loulou*, *A nos amours* and finally *Police*, span a period of thirteen years (1972–85) and form the core of Pialat's work.

References

Amiel, Vincent (2001), *Esthétique du montage*, Paris, Nathan.
Besnehard, Dominique (2003), 'Témoignages', *Cahiers du cinéma*, no. 576.
Carcassonne, Philippe (1980), 'A l'œil nu', *Cinématographe*, no. 57.
Dedet, Yann (2003), 'Témoignages', *Cahiers du cinéma*, no. 576.
Magny, Joël (1992), *Maurice Pialat*, Paris, Cahiers du cinéma.
Mermet, Gérard (1985), *Francoscopie*, Paris, Larousse.
Narboni, Jean (1979), 'Le mal est fait', *Cahiers du cinéma*, no. 304.

Pialat, Maurice (1974), 'Entretien', *La Revue du cinéma: image et son*, no. 258.

Pialat, Maurice (1974b), 'Entretien', *Positif*, no. 159.

Pialat, Maurice (1979), 'Entretien', *Cinéma 72*, no. 250.

Pialat, Maurice (1980), 'Entretien', *Cinématographe*, no. 57.

Pialat, Maurice (1984), 'Entretien', *Positif*, no. 275.

Pialat, Maurice (1984b), *A nos amours: scénario et dialogue du film*, Paris, L'Herminier.

Pialat, Maurice (2000), 'Entretien: sur la colère', *Cahiers du cinéma*, no. 550.

Powrie, Phil (1997), *French Cinema in the 1980s: Nostalgia and the Crisis of Masculinity*, Oxford, Oxford University Press.

Vincendeau, Ginette (2000), *Stars and Stardom in French Cinema*, London, Continuum.

4

Family portraits I: *Nous ne vieillirons pas ensemble, La Gueule ouverte* and *Passe ton bac d'abord*

It would certainly be valid to study Pialat's films in a variety of different combinations, to consider *L'Enfance nue, Nous ne vieillirons pas ensemble* and *La Gueule ouverte* as an autobiographical triptych stretching from childhood to maturity, for example – or to group together *La Gueule ouverte, Passe ton bac d'abord* and *A nos amours* as three variations on the theme of the breakdown of the family unit. However, I have adopted a strictly chronological approach to Pialat's films in order to suggest the sometimes subterranean connections between Pialat's films, the way unresolved (personal and aesthetic) problems carry over from one film to the next, and in order to show how problems and interpersonal conflicts that develop during the planning and filming stages of particular films become 'inscribed in the very fabric' of the film, 'both as determining factors and as reworked material' (Vincendeau 1990: 257). The division of each reading into two sections: 'Narrative and characterisation' followed by 'Form and style' is not intended to suggest a false dichotomy but merely to introduce a shift in emphasis.

Nous ne vieillirons pas ensemble (*We will not grow old together*)

Pialat considered this film 'une catharsis qu'il fallait que j'accomplisse' (Pialat 1980: 6) ('a catharsis that I would have to accomplish'), an effort to work through the trauma of a failed love affair that he had originally attempted to exorcise in a first person novel of the same title (borrowed from a poem by Paul Eluard). It was only after directing *La*

Maison des bois for French television that he had sufficient funds to envision making a film about it. He encouraged Arlette Langmann to produce a scenario based on his notes, but ultimately rewrote her work to produce what was perhaps his most detailed scenario. Later he was to regret having followed it so closely, but he initially intended to recreate the circumstances of his story as nearly as possible – down to the wallpaper in particular rooms.

Pialat did not have to go beyond family connections for crucial production funding. Jean-Pierre Rassam, who had married Anne-Marie Langmann, was impressed with Pialat's talent and wanted to produce his work. He and Pialat each contributed half the capital to found the production company, Lido Films, which financed *Nous ne vieillirons pas ensemble*. Rassam was also involved in signing Jean Yanne and Marlène Jobert for the principal roles. Determinant in the choice of Yanne was no doubt his physical resemblance to Pialat, plus Pialat had worked with him on the filming of Chabrol's *Que la bête meure* (Pialat 1974: 6). Pialat might have preferred amateurs for the other roles, but claimed he bowed to Yanne's desire to work opposite a professional actress. Jobert had been romantically linked with Claude Berri, so Pialat knew her socially and she was one of the most popular female stars of the period. He felt she would be amenable to his approach to filming.

However, as it turned out, Yanne was less understanding. Once the filming began his relationship with Pialat deteriorated rapidly and the two stopped speaking to each other. Pialat later accused Yanne of refusing to learn his part, and claimed that he deliberately attempted to sabotage the film by behaving insufferably whenever the camera was not rolling, creating an atmosphere in which it was impossible for him to do his best work as a director (Pialat 1974: 6). The situation was aggravated by the fact that Rassam took Yanne's side. Pialat and Rassam actually came to blows over the situation in a bar, one breaking a bottle over the other's head, and Rassam tried to have Pialat replaced as the director (Mérigeau 2002: 105). Pialat was able to finish the film but not without moments of considerable tension, and rumours about conflict on the set leaked into the press. The film's selection for the 1972 Cannes Film Festival did not erase Pialat's sense of betrayal. The fact that Yanne received the only prize awarded to the film at Cannes not only added insult to injury, but undercut Pialat's unflattering assessment of the star's performance. The film represented a series of firsts for Pialat: his first film with famous actors, his first effort at autobiography, his first film to be selected for the Cannes Film Festival and his first commercial success (Mérigeau 2002: 81–2; 97–102). Yet he never got over the sense that he had been stabbed in the back. Moreover, he claimed that despite the film's commercial success, he had been left with debts. His anger towards Rassam would carry over into his next film, *La Gueule ouverte* and resurface some ten years later in his attack on the 'brother-in-law' in *A nos amours*.

Narrative and characterisation

Pialat bridled when it was suggested that *Nous ne vieillirons pas ensemble* came close to being a classical French drama of adultery (Pialat 1974: 6). 'Il s'agit en gros d'un vieil adolescent inquiet de 40 ans, dont la vie professionnelle est un échec, qui abandonne sa femme qui a son âge et qui est en fait sa mère; pour vivre avec une très jeune femme qui pourrait être sa fille, qui va l'abandonner'[1] he said in an interview during the filming (Chevassu 1990: 62). This working synopsis emphasises the theme of abandonment, and suggests that the wife's role will be crucial to the drama. Instead, the final film gains in intensity by concentrating on the affair and the gradual erosion of feeling that ultimately ends it. The wife, Françoise, is not even present at the beginning of the film because Pialat, more interested in dramatic tension than narrative coherence, decided to cut the initial sequence that showed Jean taking her to the airport as she left on a trip to Russia.

The film opens with a medium shot of Jean and Catherine in bed. Catherine is awake, lying on her back facing the camera, while Jean, apparently asleep next to her, is barely visible under the sheets. The viewer might take them for a married couple if it weren't for the first words in the film, Catherine's apparently spiteful: 'J'aime pas ton appartement ... y me fout le cafard' (I don't like your apartment ... it depresses me'). This rouses Jean who grunts sleepily that it is certainly

---

1 'Broadly speaking it's about an anxious forty-year-old adolescent, unsuccessful in his profession, who leaves his wife, who is his age and actually more of a mother, to live with a very young woman who could be his daughter, who abandons him.'

as nice as her parents' place, but she demurs: 'Chez mes parents, c'est pas pareil. On sent que ce sont des gens qui s'aiment', adding after a pause 'Ici on voit bien que vous n'avez jamais rien fait pour arranger ... C'est mort, c'est pas vivant, quoi!'.[2] The plural 'vous' contributes to the ambiguity of the situation, as the viewer has no other clue to the existence of Françoise. However, the undercurrent of resentment and reproach in Catherine's remarks make it clear that the bloom is already off her relationship with Jean. In fact, as she goes on to tell him, softening visibly with the recollection, the very first time she came to the apartment, three years earlier, is her best memory of him. This might have given him pause for thought, but, as she discovers, he has fallen asleep while she was talking. Knowing Pialat's admiration for Renoir's *La Bête humaine* it is not difficult to imagine this scene as an illustration for Pecqueux's theory about love: it is always better in the beginning, when both partners are on their best behaviour. Catherine's nostalgic memorialising of her first visit to the apartment suggests, sadly, that the best is already over for her.

However, the liaison has already lasted almost six years, settling into a pattern of rendez-vous, quarrels followed by reconciliations, and departures *à deux* for weekends or vacations, that make up the bulk of the events of the film. The couple will never live together because Jean has never divorced Françoise and continues to share an apartment with her. In a sense, the entire trajectory of the film, which focuses on the period that leads to their break-up, is implicit in the initial sequence in Jean's apartment. The failed exchange in the bedroom is repeated (in a more banal guise) in the kitchen the next morning. Catherine, wrapped in a towel, joins Jean in the kitchen while he fixes his coffee, but the whine of her hairdryer drowns out his offer of toast. He is forced to repeat himself several times, but when Catherine finally understands him, she claims she is not hungry and leaves the kitchen. The next shot shows her fully dressed, pacing in the livingroom, pocketbook in hand. When Jean emerges from the kitchen, she states defiantly that she refuses to be cooped up in an apartment where she is not even allowed to stand at the window. Jean retorts that she is exaggerating, that he just does not want her 'exhibiting herself' on the balcony – out of respect for Françoise –

---

2 'At my parents it's not at all the same. You sense that they love each other [...] Here, anyone can see you [plural] haven't tried to organise things. It's dead, it's not cheerful!'

because the neighbours might talk. Not surprisingly, his considera-tion for another woman (and implicit disparagement of Catherine's vanity) fails to change her mind and once again she moves out of the frame. The camera remains on him, looking in her direction, as the door bangs.

In between this sequence and Catherine's final leave-taking, the film rehearses the couple's inevitable separation in a series of permu-tations of this departure scene. The different iterations vary the motive for the departure, the degree of emotional tension or physical violence that precedes or precipitates it, and whether it is Jean or Catherine who will leave. Pialat was well aware of the repetitive nature of these scenes, arguing that 'il ne fallait pas avoir peur de réintro-duire cinq ou six fois la même scène, très longuement, ni craindre les répétitions. On supporte bien ça en musique'[3] (Pialat 1974: 15). The different variations and the time elapsed between them establish a certain (gradually accelerating) rhythm, but also portray the gradual emotional shift that leaves Jean, the seemingly dominant partner, in the position of supplicant. As Joël Magny points out, almost the entire second half of the film involves Jean's increasingly frantic attempts to see Catherine (Magny 1992: 64). Finally, Catherine will break the pattern, disappearing without explanation and remaining absent until the penultimate scenes of the film. Then, in what is effectively the last sequence between them, she meets with Jean one last time to confirm the finality of their break-up and her engagement to someone else. Jean watches from his car as she walks away down the avenue, pausing to wave goodbye as she crosses the street. The concluding sequence, a nostalgic flashback of Catherine at the beach, represents Jean's sense of loss more powerfully than any words and seemingly completes the old pattern by having her return to him one last time. However, the deliberate overexposure of the image makes it, literally, a pale substitute for her presence – and Jean himself, present at the time, is now absent from the picture.

Although the relationship fails, it is not for lack of genuine feeling on the part of either Jean or Catherine; rather, they are 'out of synch' with each other and not in love at the same time. At forty, Jean, cynical and disillusioned about marriage, not professionally successful

---

3 'there was no need to be afraid to treat the same scene five or six times, at length, or worry about the repetition. People accept that in music'.

enough to have a steady income, is in no hurry to marry Catherine and start a family. At twenty-four, Catherine still lives with her parents and, despite having invested six years in her relationship with Jean, still worries that she will share the fate of her patron saint. The fact that she celebrates her twenty-fifth birthday in the film calls attention both to her sense of the passage of time and Jean's effort to deny the changes it brings. His primary weapon in this battle with time turns out to be a form of procrastination, a failing for which Pialat himself had some indulgence, but which has serious emotional consequences in the film. Unwilling or unable to end his failed marriage with Françoise, Jean also allows his affair with Catherine to drag on, despite the fact that this poisons his relationship with both women. Catherine admits that she was initially so in love with Jean that just seeing him made her heart pound and her knees go weak. However, by the time he offers her a ring, on her birthday – although he waits until he is about to drive away before handing her the small box – she refuses it, stabbing him with the admission that she now loves him less. Yet she struggles to repress tears as she explains that the change in her feelings has occurred little by little. From this point on she will begin to distance herself from him emotionally. As she withdraws, he pursues her, finally reproaching her for failing to respond to his change of heart: 'j' t'ai jamais aimé avant. Et main-tenant que je m'aperçois que je t'aime, tu t'en vas' (Pialat 1973: 26) ('I never loved you before. And now that I realise that I love you, you're leaving').

Jean's reproach, outrageous, and so self-serving that it would be laughable, were it not also cruel, is actually one of the more subtle ways in which he is abusive. Although taciturn, he is capable of outbursts that are tantamount to assaults. The core of sequence twelve consists of the two-minute tirade in which he tells Catherine he wants to end their relationship and disparages her as ugly, ordinary and vulgar. His attack is the more stunning because it appears totally unprovoked and Catherine does not respond, waiting mutely for the storm to pass. Yet it is not merely the verbal attacks on Catherine that led some critics to consider the film misogynist. Jean is also physically abusive, his potential for violence suggested by moments in early sequences where he angrily grabs and pushes or shoves Catherine away. The violence escalates later during a weekend at the beach when he terrifies her by ripping her T-shirt in anger and frustration because she evinces no interest in making love. More shocking still, because akin to rape, is his struggle with her – on the eve of her birthday – as he attempts to take off her underpants in order to verify that she has not slept with someone else. Pialat called the action both 'indecent' and 'obscene' (Pialat 1980: 6) however, his conception of the scene was far more sordid than its actual execution. As the couple's struggle was filmed in a medium shot and in quasi darkness, the viewer sees Catherine's resistance, without seeing or comprehending the nature of Jean's attack on her.

What saves the film from being truly misogynist is Jean's emotional dependence on and genuine feeling for both Catherine and his wife. The latter will actually intercede for him with Catherine's parents in the hope of bringing about a reconciliation. It is this gesture, motivated by her affection for her husband and her sympathy for his distress, that Pialat had intended to make the focal point of the film. Yet her apparently selfless action is counterbalanced by a later monologue – delivered when Jean is emotionally at his lowest ebb after learning of Catherine's engagement – in which she brings up a host of old resentments and accuses him of being a womaniser like his father. In fact, taken as a whole, the film suggests that the bond that links Pialat's couples grows out of a shared past but is forged as much by pain, disappointment and resentment as love. Catherine's struggle to distance herself from Jean reflects the intensity of this bond, and her final flight suggests that she does not entirely trust herself not to slip back into their old pattern. However, her decision to break with Jean also reveals a strength of will belied by her physical fragility. If she, like Jean – and his wife – compel the viewer's sympathy at various points, Pialat's insistence on his characters' shallowness, their vulgarity and their baser instincts suggests the tenor of his realism and provides some justification for critics' labelling it sordid or naturalist.

Style and form

By contrast, the film itself seems almost stylised, closer to Racine than Zola's naturalism in its paring away of extraneous detail to focus on the period when the couple's relationship founders. The film unfolds as a succession of arrivals and departures, exits and entrances, staged primarily in transitional spaces: streets, cars, train and Metro stations or hotel rooms. Only the small village where Jean goes to visit his father, or that of Saint Paterne (referred to only as Saint Pat) in Indre et Loire where Catherine visits her grandmother, convey some sense of place and of history, but they serve only as a backdrop for the couple's story. In fact, Pialat's use of transitional spaces suggests an erosion of the family and social connections that anchor the individual in the collectivity, and were crucial to Zola's portrayal of French society. While there are appearances by Catherine's parents, her grandmother, Jean's father, and Catherine's brother and sister-in-law, the viewer gets very little sense of the social universe in which Jean and Catherine live. Moreover, neither is clearly affiliated with a particular professional milieu, even though the viewer is given a glimpse of Jean at work editing a film, and he evokes parties at which he introduced Catherine to other filmmakers.

The paucity of 'naturalist' detail is matched by a general lack of visual interest in many scenes where Jean and Catherine are together. The early sequence in Camargue is an exception, but even the couple's walks on the beach or their afternoon in the park provide only a more scenic frame for their exchanges. The repetition of similar sequences tempted Jacques Kermabon to reduce them to a formula: a long shot in which one character emerges from the background, then moves to the foreground and engages a second character in conversation (Kermabon 1983: 52). The most frequently repeated of such sequences begins as a view of a street or parking area shot through Jean's windscreen as he spies Catherine and hails her. She comes towards him and gets in the car. They are then filmed in a two shot as they talk, framed in the shallow space of the car's interior. The final scene between them merely reverses this pattern. The visual monotony creates tension as the viewer exhausts the visual field and remains trapped within it, doubly trapped because the body of the car creates a frame within the frame. In the case of Catherine, also framed by Jean's windscreen or rear-view mirror as she comes into or leaves the space of the image, the motif suggests a form of capture or possession which becomes increasingly figurative and nostalgic. The pattern is broken with Jean's final flashback where the frame disappears and Catherine floats free, literally and figuratively. This flashback is an anomaly in Pialat's work but emphasises the overall nostalgic tone of the film, already evident in the very first sequence. It also calls attention to the importance of time in a film where the passage of time brings inevitable loss. The sense of time passing, associated in the film with both the monotony and the anguish of waiting, is intensified by formal repetitions and underlined by Pialat's use of *plan-séquences*.

Pialat initially saw the *plan-séquence* as a way of portraying events with a maximum of intensity and authenticity, capturing the actors' interactions and allowing a scene to develop fully without artificially breaking it into discrete shots. However, he discovered that it also provided him with a technique to suggest the passage of time: 'Avec les plans-séquences, j'avais découvert que je pouvais, en un temps qui n'était pas le temps réel, donner l'illusion de l'écoulement du temps'[4] (Pialat 1980b: 29). Although a sense of lost or wasted time assumes considerable importance (and a variety of guises) in Pialat's career: deferral or delay of his projects, false starts, and his own procrastination among them, *Nous ne vieillirons pas ensemble* is the first of his films in which the passage of time becomes both a theme and a formal element. In fact, one of Pialat's disappointments in making *Nous ne vieillirons pas ensemble* was that he could not recapture the emotional intensity of certain events when he attempted to recreate them in the film: 'on ne peut pas faire une chose autobiographique à chaud, et puis on a vieilli'[5] (Pialat 1980: 6). The element of time remains crucial to his work, if only through his effort to erase explicit temporal references from his films and to situate his subjects, even in period films such *Van Gogh* or *Sous le soleil de Satan*, in an indeterminate present that would give them a sense of immediacy.

Pialat considered *Nous ne vieillirons pas ensemble* a crucial point in his career, a moment when he might have opted to become a more commercial filmmaker. Yet the sense that he was betrayed, by his principal actor, his producer and ultimately the film community, led him to withdraw and then (almost defiantly) to undertake the most personal and the least commercially successful film of his career, *La Gueule ouverte*.

---

4 'With long takes I discovered that I could, in a time frame that was not real time, give the illusion of the passage of time.'
5 'you can't do something autobiographical immediately, 'while it's hot', and then you are older'.

La Gueule ouverte ('Mouth Agape')

The project that became *La Gueule ouverte* took shape in 1971 when Pialat was marking time, unable to begin filming *Nous ne vieillirons pas ensemble* because his stars had to fulfil other contractual obligations. Discussing various projects with Berri and Rassam led him to consider an adaptation of Henri Graziani's *Le Fils* (*The Son*), the story of a man who returns to his childhood home because his mother is dying. Yet Pialat quickly realised that he could never film Graziani's story because it conflicted with his memories of his own mother's death some twelve years earlier. Reworking the subject led to a thirty-page script that he eventually tossed into a drawer convinced that any film that focused on a dying woman for an hour and a half was hopeless.

After finishing *Nous ne vieillirons pas ensemble* he took a second look at the project. He perhaps willingly courted disaster in deciding to make the film, investing himself and his production company in what he later called 'a suicidal subject' – 'un sujet suicidaire' (Pialat 1980: 7). Yet it was of crucial importance to him: 'Quand ma mère est morte, c'est ce qui m'a le plus frappé dans ma vie, je ne crois pas qu'il y ait un œdipe quelconque là-dedans'[6] (Pialat 1980: 7). His concern over his father's failing health undoubtedly also influenced his decision, as Antoine (known as Roger) Pialat was in a retirement home in Cunlhat – not far from where *La Gueule ouverte* was filmed – and he died before the film was completed.

Pialat intended the film to be both powerful and shocking. 'Je parlerai vraiment de la mort, d'une façon scandaleuse. On dira "toi, tu crèves, moi je vis". Aujourd'hui la crudité est nécessaire,'[7] he told interviewers at *Positif* (Pialat 1974: 6). The title of the film itself, which might be roughly translated as 'mouth agape', reflects his willingness to shock, although the scene that was to have justified it – in which the father and the son find it impossible to close the deceased mother's mouth after her jaw drops open – does not figure in the film. Pialat recalled that Hubert Deschamps (who played the father) and Philippe Léotard alternated between total repulsion and hysterical laughter,

6 'When my mother died, that was the thing that hit me the hardest in my whole life, I don't think there was anything oedipal about it.'

7 'I will really talk about death in a scandalous way. People will say: "you're going to die and I'm alive". Crudeness is a necessary thing today.'

never able to complete the scene. Pialat even went so far as to attempt to shoot a scene in his family mausoleum, scandalising some of the crew by having his mother's casket opened. This scene never appears in the film because the narrow space and poor lighting made it almost impossible to shoot, and Pialat, reconsidering, decided the material was unusable and destroyed it.

Yet despite Pialat's almost Flaubertian determination to portray the grim realities of the mother's physical decline and death, he originally envisioned a balance between eros and thanatos that would require giving equal time to the son's amorous adventures. The son's libido was to increase in inverse proportion to his mother's decline, as though his desire could deny death, both hers and ultimately his own. However, most of the scenes concerning the son's sexual escapades were either never made, or were cut during the editing, leaving the mother's death as the film's sole dramatic focus. Pialat's evident willingness to go as far as possible in restaging certain of his memories notwithstanding, the film rises above autobiography to present the death of a parent as a universal human experience. *La Gueule ouverte* is a major, if difficult, work that demands the viewer recognise film as a medium capable of producing a reflection on the human condition as powerful as Rembrandt's studies of the elderly, or as fearless as the painter's late self-portraits, which show signs of his approaching senility.

Narrative and characterisation

Like Pialat's earlier films, *La Gueule ouverte* is a fragmented linear narrative vectored by the movement of the characters, but primarily the son, Philippe, between Paris, where Philippe and his wife live, and the small town in Auvergne where Philippe's father – sometimes referred to as 'le garçu' – owns a small shop. Yet despite the constant references to movement, arrivals and departures, the *plan séquences* follow the characters' efforts to kill time as they wait for the inevitable, when the inevitable can neither be hurried nor delayed.

The film opens, emblematically, as Philippe sits alone in an empty hospital waiting room. The next sequence shows Monique, his mother, undergoing a cobalt radiation treatment. The silence is broken only by the hospital attendants' voices as they tell her to climb upon the table and to breathe normally. As they adjust the machinery above her head, switching off the light, the machine hums and a luminous graduated scale used to position the equipment is projected briefly onto Monique's face, giving her head the look of a skull and conveying almost subliminally what Philippe will finally put into words much later, that Monique's case is terminal.

The anxiety generated by these first sequences is initially dissipated by the apparent normalcy of the next scene, a justly famous eight-and-a-half minute sequence that begins as Philippe shuts a window and turns to sit down at the table where he and his mother are finishing lunch. They are filmed in a medium two shot, sitting side by side, facing the camera rather than each other. Refilling his wine glass, Philippe congratulates his mother on her appetite, claiming, as she helps herself to some yoghurt, that she has eaten more than he has. As she consumes the yoghurt, spoonful after slow spoonful, looking down at the table and scraping the bottom of the container, she changes the subject, admonishing Philippe about how lucky he is to have a wife like Nathalie. At this, Philippe darts a wary glance in her direction, and, taking some grapes, pops one into his mouth as though to block any temptation to respond. As he chews on the grapes, she relates that Nathalie has told her that he was unfaithful. Still looking down, ostensibly at the yoghurt, she concludes 'je pensais que pour ça du moins tu ne tenais pas de ton père' ('I thought that at least in that respect you didn't resemble your father'). Here Philippe reacts by taking the offensive: 'Encore jalouse à ton âge! A Montreuil tu me traînais dans les bistrots le soir quand il ne rentrait pas'.[8] He prods her to remember how she spat on a picture of Gene Tierney that his father had cut out of a movie magazine because it resembled one of his mistresses. And finally, he accuses her of cheating too – and perhaps plotting a divorce. Smiling faintly, she brushes off the charge with 'tu inventes' ('you are making that up'), claiming she could have hardly had an affair since he was such a fearful, anxious child he always wanted to be with her. It is clear that each has a different version of the family story – they even disagree completely about her father, whom she saw as an ogre, while her son adored him.

8 'Still jealous at your age! You used to drag me around to all the bars at night when he didn't come home.'

One of the most striking features of this highly loaded exchange is the fact that neither ever meets the other's gaze (Magny 1992: 62). Although Philippe frequently looks over at his mother as he addresses her, she is either looking down at the yoghurt, or gazing unfocusedly ahead. For Magny, the mother's avoidance of her son's gaze is the clearest sign that she is afraid that it will confirm her suspicions that she is doomed. The seriousness of her condition suffices to explain why Philippe ends a conversation that pits them against each other. He gets up from the table and puts on a recording of Mozart's *Cosi fan tutti*, cutting her off as she airs her resentment about her father's treatment of her as a child – an old story that he has no doubt heard before and clearly has little sympathy with. The two of them sit 'listening' together, for two and a half minutes of real time during which nothing is heard but the Mozart recording, although a repeated 'adio' 'adio' resonates with connotations not intended by Mozart. Philippe fidgets and smokes, while his mother continues to gaze straight ahead as though lost in thought. As the lovers' duet ends and is followed by a chorus, the absence of any action creates a tension that continues to build, then breaks as the phone rings. Philippe answers, turning the music down rather than off, but as he waits silently to be transferred to someone else, his mother resumes her complaints about her father as though she had never been interrupted, suggesting that she is more preoccupied by past resentments than her present fate. After he hangs up, Philippe's announcement that he has been offered a job in television ends the meal, but his pleasure seems lost on his mother who fails to congratulate him, looking at him directly for the first time only to express concern that he will lose his other job. Then as she rises from the table she sways off balance; Philippe will barely catch her before she falls. She quickly recovers and moves out of the frame, but the next time the viewer sees her she will be in the hospital.

This sequence conveys all the complexity of the family universe that Pialat portrays, in which none of the members has full confidence in the others and expressions of sympathy, affection and concern are freighted with ambivalence and suppressed rancour over old grievances, never really acknowledged, pardoned or resolved. Each of the family members is both victim and victimiser in a larger family drama that covers more than one generation. Neither mother, father nor son is presented as particularly admirable – in fact, it becomes clear during the exchange between Monique and Philippe that all three of them secretly stole money from the small shop they had owned in Paris, ultimately bankrupting their own business. Similarly Monique's illness will use up the last of the emotional capital that unites the family members, her death leading to the break-up of the family. Following this sequence, the film moves inexorably towards her death, the funeral and departure that will end the film.

Philippe, returning to their apartment in the early morning hours, wakes his wife to announce that he has spoken to the doctor and Monique has only a few months to live. Nathalie, suspicious and resentful about his absence, does not attempt to console him, claiming that surely he must have expected this, sooner or later. However, when the two appear at the hospital in the next sequence bringing flowers, Monique appears radiant with happiness, announcing that she has received a letter from 'le garçu' who will arrive shortly. When he does, she confides that she is better off at the hospital as the couple was always fighting and Philippe had accused her of using him as a taxi service. Yet if she is better off, and only expresses some doubts about her condition, small milestones mark her continuing deterioration. Finally the doctor, cruelly professional, tells Philippe that nothing further can be done. Monique will return home, arriving in Auvergne in semi-darkness and be carried on a stretcher into the bedroom of the house behind *La Maison de la laine*, rapidly ceasing to function as a character and becoming the central prop for the action. She will figure in many sequences, only her head visible below the blue chair rail (although some indications suggest she was filmed in different rooms), almost lost in the expanse of highly patterned wallpaper that dominates the room – compositions that recall the claustrophobic interiors painted by Vuillard.

Both Philippe and his father escape this increasingly oppressive space by fleeing to bars and amorous rendez-vous. Pialat reinforces the resemblance between them by having Philippe flirt with two young women who come to visit or help with his mother, then showing his father accosting the same two women in the street as he returns to the house in the next sequence. Roger pats the closest one on the bottom, adding with pathetic ribaldry 'pas besoin de Vaseline' ('no need for Vaseline'). Yet the incredible crudity of this remark is counterbalanced by the extraordinary patience and unexpected refine-ments of tenderness he shows in caring for his incapacitated wife –

tossing away the napkin he has used as a bib while feeding her and getting a clean napkin out of the armoire just to wipe off her mouth. If, frustrated and depressed, he declares angrily to Nathalie that he wants it to be over, she is nonetheless touched by his devotion. Moreover, as Joël Magny points out, he is the only character who never avoids looking at Monique directly, even though, cruelly, her last words to him before she lapses into a vegetative state sum up years of jealousy, neglect, anger and humiliation: 'Tu traînes avec une gueuse ... Tu ... sens ... le ... vin'.[9]

Where Philippe dominates the early scenes in Paris, once Monique returns to Auvergne, Roger will play an increasingly important role in the film. There were practical reasons for this – Hubert Deschamps was, to Pialat's great irritation, involved in another film during the shooting of the earlier sequences and was constantly leaving the set. Moreover, the fact that Nathalie Baye and Philippe Léotard were at the time romantically involved complicated Pialat's efforts to develop the erotic dimension of the son's role. Nor is it negligible that Philippe Léotard was in essence playing Pialat's character – and that the director's dissatisfaction with his work also contributed to the increasing importance of the father's role.

It is Roger who watches over his wife's last moments and announces her death to his son, reading in an adjacent room. Grief-stricken, Roger will break down completely as Monique's coffin is closed, and during the dinner that follows the funeral, he does not participate in the strained, banal conversation, escaping briefly into the adjacent bar where he orders another glass of wine, and breaks down again, sobbing to the bartender that he and his wife had been together for thirty-four years. In the final sequence, Nathalie and Philippe argue with him as they head out the door of the shop to drive back to Paris, but he is unwilling to accompany them, insisting that he remain 'près d'elle' ('close to her'). Exasperated by his stubborn refusal, the couple leaves without him, a long tracking shot showing the receding view of the town in the gathering darkness from the back of their car. Then the final shot cuts back to the shop where Roger is turning off the lights; the credits appear as we hear the final click and the screen goes black.

The final blackness reflects the film's bleak pessimism. It is not

9 'You are playing around with a tramp ... You ... smell ... of ... wine'.

merely the terrible sadness of the mother's premature death and her loneliness within the family circle where her illness will finally completely isolate her, or even the painful irony that her husband's expressions of love and devotion, his unwillingness to leave her, come far too late. It is in fact, now too late for all of them, and each fails the others. As if to underline the shared guilt, the father's earlier abandonment of his wife and son is echoed by his own abandonment by his son and daughter-in-law after the funeral. Pialat had intended to carry the symmetry even further by including a violent argument between Philippe and Nathalie in the final sequence that would have clearly shown the breakdown of their own marriage, but the scene was never shot. Its absence preserves the focus on the mother's death, which is portrayed as both banal and horrible.

Style and form

'Peu de films sont aussi audacieux que *la Gueule ouverte*' ('Few films are as bold as *La Gueule ouverte*'), a critic at *Cinématographe* told Pialat (Pialat 1980: 8). This boldness is both a product of Pialat's conception of his subject and the strikingly original way it is treated. Pialat takes up precisely those aspects of the subject that most filmmakers would avoid, focusing on the mother's physical deterioration and drawing out her final days as Roger and Philippe are reduced to watching and pacing back and forth, listening to her increasingly laboured breathing and final death rattles. Pialat comes closest in this film to his ideal of making a film in as few shots as possible. By his count the film had only 80 shots, compared with the already parsimonious 120 for *Nous ne vieillirons pas ensemble*, while *Passe ton bac d'abord* would have more than 600. The long takes not only slow the rhythm of the film but give it an almost documentary quality, forcing the viewer to follow even the most trivial actions. This documentary quality is underscored by the authenticity of the décor (Pialat merely rented a large furnished house in Auvergne, thus sparing himself the expense of a decorator) and cameo appearances by the townspeople. Notable among them are the café owner and his wife, who fumbles her lines as she expresses her sympathy to Roger; the neighbour who has a drink in the kitchen and launches self-consciously into a monologue about his garden and shopping in the local market – and the wedding procession of an immigrant family that passes by, to Roger's astonishment, as he is about to cross the street to the bar. Yet for all the seemingly digressive, purely anecdotal quality of these brief cameos, they are crucial to the film, linking the family to the larger community of provincial society and opposing the life of the community to the mother's death, just as the marriage procession serves as a formal counterpoint to the funeral procession.

Surprisingly then, Pialat himself felt the film was entirely too Bressonian: 'C'est un film assez froid et dont les qualités reposent pour une bonne part sur l'esthétique' he told interviewers at *Positif* (Pialat 1974: 13) ('It's a rather cold film and its merits are for the most part aesthetic'). Certainly, despite Pialat's daring use of Mozart to replace what is not said between Philippe and his mother, silence plays as important a role in *La Gueule ouverte* as in any of Bresson's films. The father and son's pacing in the concluding sequences functions as a motif similar to Bresson's use of doors and staircases. Moreover Pialat's elimination of specific temporal indications and anecdotal information about his characters (we learn little about Philippe or Nathalie's profession) gives the film an almost timeless dimension characteristic of Bresson's work. However, Pialat's formal preoccupations also take him further in the direction of documentary representation: the desire to film his characters in full shots, a greater use of natural lighting and a particular attention to sound.

If Pialat disliked calling attention to the formal qualities of his work, he nonetheless relies on formal elements rather than dialogue to convey certain ideas and complex emotions. The clash between eros and thanatos – and the promised 'toi, tu crèves, moi, je vis,' which was never voiced in the film – is represented with far greater subtlety and complexity in a single surprising cut that links Philippe, lying alone in bed berating himself after an erotic fiasco, to his mother, in pain in her hospital bed. Particularly striking, however, given the static quality of the film, is the formal contrast provided by two extended travelling shots. In the first – over two minutes in duration – the camera inches forward around the dark flank of the village church, gradually revealing the long line of mourners standing in the street waiting to express their condolences to the Bastide family. It is an iconic representation of the rituals of death and mourning – a cinematic equivalent of Courbet's composition for *Burial at Ornans* – enhanced by the fact that the only sound is the tolling of church bells.

The second of these shots is the stunning minute-and-a-half tracking shot filmed as Philippe and Nathalie drive away after the funeral. Pialat claimed that this shot violated his own principles as he normally avoided setting up the camera in unexpected places, and here the camera was placed in the boot of the car (Pialat 1974: 13). Done hastily because in five minutes it would have been dark, the shot prolongs the couple's departure by stretching it out, framing the shop, then the small sidestreets, then the main highway, bordered by stands of trees that increase the effect of the growing darkness. The only sounds are other passing cars and the motor that slows as the car leaves the narrower sidestreets, then gears up as it enters the highway. Marc Vernet analysed the 'violence' of this shot as it is expressed through its structural tensions: the nostalgia of the image, focused on what remains behind, countering the forward dynamic of the shot; the constant metamorphosis of the image played off against the static frame; the elasticity of the shot versus the sense of being torn away (Vernet 1991: 139). It becomes a visual equivalent for the son's state of mind, torn between, on the one hand, grief over his mother's death and guilt over leaving his father behind; and on the other his desire to put death and the past behind him, to live and to escape into his own future. Yet the forward drive of the image is broken by the final sequence, which takes us back to the father, alone in his shop in the darkness.

Despite a favourable critical reception, it is perhaps not surprising that the film drew only a small audience, just under 27,000 in all of France, while *Nous ne vieillirons pas ensemble* had brought in over a million and a half viewers. Pialat's losses forced the liquidation of his production company. Although this was certainly not the end of his career, the bankruptcy inevitably awakened old memories of the loss of the family business in Montreuil. It would be four years before he made another film.

Passe ton bac d'abord ('Pass your exams first')

Pialat called it a film 'qui ne devrait pas être fait' ('that should never have been made') and it was in fact a film of last resort. Eked out on a very slim budget, it was the result of the pressure to produce a film, any film, after he had spent advance money and signed a coproduction agreement with the television channel France 3 in 1976. The advances were for another film entirely, a film entitled *Les Filles du faubourg*, based on an autobiographical scenario by Arlette Langmann. However, as Pialat worked on Langmann's scenario, his doubts about the project grew. He worried that the budget would not be adequate to do a period film (the action was set in the 1960s) and foresaw difficulties in casting the various parts.

Another subject appealed to him considerably more. 'Les Meurtrières' ('The Murderesses') – its working title – was based on an incident that had attracted considerable public attention four years earlier. Two adolescent girls hitchhiking in the countryside attempted to rob the man who picked them up and then stabbed him to death. Pialat went so far as to write a preliminary script, engage a cast and crew and set a date to begin filming – fully intending to present this film to his producer and distributor instead of *Les Filles du faubourg*. When he did finally apprise them of the change in plans, the day before filming was to begin, they were stunned (Pialat 1984: 131). Pialat went ahead with his plan – but after two days of delays and technical problems he abandoned the shoot, fearing that without the full support of his backers he risked real catastrophe (Mérigeau 2002: 142). After the failure of his own production company, he could not afford to acquire the reputation of a director who bankrupted his producers. He was now in a very difficult situation, much of the advance money was gone, and there was no way to reimburse his backers. He would have to make a film with the 700,000F that remained.

He began to consider making a sequel to *L'Enfance nue* – based on the adolescent adventures of 'Josette' and her boyfriend, who, like François, had been a foster child. The couple agreed to play themselves in the film, but just two weeks before the filming was to begin they had second thoughts. Pialat had to replace them with professionals, Sabine Haudepin (Elisabeth) and Philippe Marlaud (Philippe), although neither corresponded exactly to the characters he had imagined. The rest of the cast, with few exceptions (the café owner, the philosophy professor, Elisabeth's mother) was made up of amateurs, mostly students from working-class families who, like their characters, spent much of their free time hanging out at the local café, 'Le Caron'. Arlette Langmann worked on the script – a day at a time – drawing on the adolescents' experiences and their interactions. As in *L'Enfance nue*, the line between film and reality blurs as each of the actors (except Sabine) uses his or her own name. The filming ran through most of January while temperatures hovered just above zero – the freezing temperatures reflected in some of the film's action – then Pialat ran out of money. It was May before he could get financing and regroup to resume work, but he then completed almost the whole second half of the film in about ten days (Pialat 1979: 60). As Sabine Haudepin and Philippe Marlaud were not free for the May shooting, their characters disappear from the film, their absence justified by their decision to run away from Lens. By the film's conclusion, their story has become just one of the stories of a group of young, not quite adults whose frustration at the few choices offered them – even if they were to pass their exams – becomes emblematic of an entire class.

Narrative and characterisation

Passe ton bac d'abord opens as the credits run against a view of the graffiti decorating a school desktop: ANARCHIE in large letters first dominates the visual field, and then in slightly smaller letters the verb AIME. There are stick figures, one with a dunce cap, hearts, an artfully drawn boxer, a telephone – the doodled figures turning the desktop into an amateur Miró. As at the beginning of *L'Enfance nue,* the soundtrack during the credits will be reprised later in the film: the sound of a door closing, students taking their places, then finally the voice of the philosophy professor, advising students to begin by discarding all of their preconceived notions about the study of philosophy. The opening of the film then coincides with the first day of the school year – and by the film's conclusion it is clear that the timeframe for the events is roughly the last year before the baccalaureate examination.

A handful of main characters emerge: Elisabeth, who opens the first sequence at 'Le Caron' by walking into the frame from the right eating a handful of fries. The next shot shows Bernard sitting at another table next to Cathy, asking for advice on how to break up with his girlfriend Karine as Patrick, his closest male friend, provides running commentary for a newcomer, Philippe. Two other girls, one blonde, one brunette, round out the group. As later sequences indicate, both are avidly pursued by the owner of 'Le Caron'. If there is only a glimpse of the pert, blond Agnès, the viewer learns from

Patrick that, like Cathy and the about to be dumped Karine, 'elle aime surtout Bernard' ('she mostly likes Bernard').

Pialat provides an almost classic exposition, where the multiplicity of characters is rendered less confusing because they are associated with types: Bernard, the young Don Juan – 'il les aime toutes' ('he loves them all') as Patrick explains to Philippe; Bernard's older counterpart will be the owner of 'Le Caron', 'le vieux dragueur' ('the old flirt'). Elisabeth fits most neatly the stereotype of the 'easy' girl, who will discover her true love in Philippe. Patrick, with his transparent moustache, takes on the role of detached observer and go-between. Presenting himself as worldly wise and cynical, he dismisses all of the girls as unattractive and denounces Elisabeth in particular as a 'petite pute' ('a little whore'). However, his capacity for astonishment – and his astonishment at Philippe's attraction to Elisabeth in this early sequence – reveals his vulnerability. In fact, if the characters do approach types, this being the source of much of the humour in the film, their characters – like their comings and goings – are by no means wholly predictable. Patrick's heated attack on Elisabeth suggests his own attraction to her, and she is in fact the only girl he will be associated with in the course of the film – other than his younger sister Valérie. Even Philippe, cast in the role of Elisabeth's 'true love', indulges in a brief flirtation with Agnès.

Each of the main characters has a particular presence: Bernard's hoarse speech and his half-strangled laugh; his ironic use of 'une chance' ('a piece of luck'), his prankish physicality – he swoops Agnès off her chair at 'Le Caron' and carries her away giggling, pulls her onto his lap at her wedding and teases her with the eels that her new husband keeps in their bathtub. Philippe, seemingly more mature, more serious, notices Elisabeth, immediately moves to form a couple with her, lecturing her on her smoking, her aimlessness and her habit of staring at men in the street. Patrick's jaded attitude contrasts with his strong sense of propriety – only he will wear formal attire at Agnès' wedding. He tends to end his sentences with 'eh' and the rising pitch of his voice serves as a barometer for his shock or surprise. Agnès, despite other flirtations, gravitates toward Bernard like a small planet, even seeking him out at her wedding. Other characters, less developed, like the childfaced blonde in the group, are typed as having a 'petit cul' ('little backside') particularly attractive to the café owner, or in the case of her brunette counterpart, by a cynicism mitigated by frequent yawns and chronic sleepiness – caused by the fact that she gets up at 3 o'clock in the morning to work in the textile mills at Roubaix.

The characters are also typed by their decision about whether to remain in Lens after finishing school. Patrick's desire to leave is clear from the very first sequence. Agnès, unlucky in love, will stay, settling for an older boy, Rocky, already established as a truckdriver. As she explains to Bernard when she announces her intention to get married (clearly hoping this will galvanise him into expressing his feelings for her): 'Le mariage pour moi c'est un peu une planque' ('Marriage for me is a kind of refuge'). She cannot conceive of leaving: 'partir de chez moi? Pour aller où?' ('Leave home? To go where?') she says incredulously when Bernard suggests this might be an alternative to marrying Rocky.

Philippe's situation is more complicated; he never knew his father, as he tells the group when they settle in a room above 'Le Caron' to eat and smoke. He hated the orphanage – his frequent attempts to run away ending in failure. His story is received with considerable hilarity by his listeners, particularly as – apparently engrossed in his own story – he loses his balance and pitches forward off the edge of his seat right in the middle of it. However, it is clear that his relationship with Elisabeth and her parents provides him with a substitute family. Bernard, whose relationship with his own father is not the most cordial, considers Philippe's lack of family ties 'une chance' and makes it clear that he will leave Lens at the first opportunity. He invites Patrick to leave with him, suggesting that they visit Patrick's supposedly rich aunt in Paris.

The viewer gets only brief fragmentary glimpses of the group's family life, the major sections focusing on Elizabeth and Patrick, although there is also a short sequence filmed at Bernard's where he is called to lunch by his exasperated mother. He crawls sleepily out of bed in the alcove of the dormer room he probably shares with his two younger siblings, then joins them at the kitchen table where his mother serves him with equal helpings of food and reproach. His father, a former miner suffering from silicosis, never appears on camera. As Bernard describes him to Frédérique, a girl he meets at the beach: 'il a attrapé un sale caractère parce qu'il ne peut pas sentir sa maladie' ('He has become really difficult because he can't stand being sick').

On the other hand, Elisabeth's situation is visibly better. The family lives in a small house; her father has some important social connections. Her older sister is married and employed, paying her share of the family meals when she eats at home, although she may not have passed her exams. She decries their value, claiming that even people who have their *bac* end up in unskilled jobs. Elisabeth's parents take her behaviour in stride, tolerating her numerous boyfriends – and her sexual activity – saying little, even when she announces to her father 'je l'aurai pas mon bac, j'fous plus rien' ('I won't pass, I'm not doing any studying'). They receive Philippe, the first boy she has ever brought home, tactfully and then affectionately, treating him, to Elisabeth's surprise (and momentary pique) as a son-in-law before the fact. He chats comfortably with Elisabeth's mother when Elisabeth is not there, opening a cabinet to help himself to a lump of sugar. He even does the dinner dishes while the rest of the family sits at the table.

Elisabeth's impulsive decision to run away could only have been motivated by the extraordinary argument that follows Agnès's wedding, where the slightly drunk Philippe makes a scene because Elisabeth is dancing too closely to Bernard. Apparently afraid that her daughter will break up with Philippe, to whom she is genuinely attached, Elisabeth's mother insults her and blames her for preci- pitating the trouble. The intensity of this argument, entirely scripted rather than improvised, according to Pialat, seems excessive, although it prefigures the hysterical exchanges between mother and daughter in *A nos amours*. Nothing in the mother's earlier quiet demeanour and her obvious affection for Elisabeth (whose characteristic gesture of putting her head on her mother's shoulder suggests that she returns it) prepares the viewer for the intensity of the scene. When Elisabeth responds to the verbal assault by declaring that her mother probably wishes she could sleep with Philippe herself, the mother falls apart, threatens suicide and attempts to swallow pills, while Elisabeth, screaming 'arrête ton cinéma' ('stop this show') tries to wrest them away from her, then runs out the door. The scene concludes with a shot of the mother looking out the window, watching Elisabeth run down the road towards town and 'Le Caron'. A last brief sequence at 'Le Caron', where Philippe finds her alone at a table, leads to their departure, which marks a decisive break in the narrative.

The next sequence opens with an extremely romantic shot of a girl riding down the beach on a white horse, her long dark hair blowing in the wind. Several months have apparently passed as it is no longer winter, in fact, this is not Lens nor is the girl a familiar character. However, Bernard rapidly comes into the picture; he is apparently camping on the beach and the first shot represents both his point of view and the considerable attraction of this new girl. Another shot reveals Agnès checking his tent and wondering at his absence, then knocking on the various doors in the camper, parked in the dunes, where the others are sleeping the morning away. The beach sequences unfold on the theme of comic seduction, as Bernard takes up with the new girl, Frédérique – giving lucky Patrick the chance to ride her horse.

Meanwhile the owner of 'Le Caron', apparently also on vacation, spies his two favourites buying postcards, takes up with them and perhaps hoping for more, invites them to lunch, only to end up paying the restaurant bill for the entire group. This brief escape to the beach contrasts the bright open area of the shore with the oppressive industrial landscape of Lens and highlights the differences in lifestyle between the bourgeoise, Frédérique, and the rest of group.

Bernard, attempting to rendez-vous with her (accompanied by faithful sidekick Patrick) has to wait for her to get out of mass. She has a car – primly putting on her glasses before she drives off with them – and lives in a large summer beach home where she later invites Bernard to her equally large room to listen to punk rock. She then propositions him, revealing as she undresses a teddy printed with a huge tiger's head, its teeth bared in a savage snarl. In the final beach sequence, Bernard, having perhaps stolen it from her, will wave his trophy in front of the others as 'la peau de la bête' ('the skin of the beast'). These sequences underline Frédérique's otherness, and the bourgeois notions of property and propriety associated with her are coupled with an almost Chabrolian – if it were not treated farcically – evocation of the predatory self-interest masked by bourgeois manners. Yet it is also no doubt her difference – and the fact that he will perhaps never see her again – that leads Bernard to talk to her most openly about his feelings towards his father, confessing that if they do not get along it is really his fault.

The sequence immediately following the events at the Camping at Bray-Dunes provides an external view of Lens, even though it abruptly takes the viewer back into the mining town with a long shot of a Rolls-

Royce slowly driving down a street between two identical rows of sombre brick houses, the image accompanied by strains of classical music. A young man in a suit looking out the window tries, unsuccessfully, to get directions to 'la rue des Rosiers' ('the street of rosebushes'). The next long shot of the rows of houses reveals more of a grim industrial landscape behind them, underlining the irony. Dogs bark at the strangers, and as the car stops in front of Patrick's home and the two young men get out, the camera stays on the car, shifting to frame its imposing front grille and its Paris licence plate. Nothing could express disdain for the wealth and class privilege it symbolises more than the small neighbourhood dog that trots out and lifts a leg to baptise the left front tyre.

The two men have arrived to invite Valérie, whom they apparently met at 'Le Caron', to pose for a series of fashion photographs. They attempt to convince Valérie's manifestly dubious parents that the proposition is both serious and honourable. It will be rejected out of hand by her father. Their final polite goodbye is directed at Valérie who watches, wordless, her face blank, as what appears to be a chance to escape Lens walks out the front door. Patrick berates his father for not allowing her to take it – 'tu es jeune, toi, tu connais tout' ('You're young, you know everything') his father retorts. While the dog might well be a symbolic stand-in for Pialat himself, the sequence is not wholly one sided in its implicit attack on the rich. Pialat makes visible the stultifying grimness that fuels Valérie's (and Patrick's) dreams of escape – just as we see the shallowness of their dreams of wealth and glamour. Nor in fact do the parents compel our entire sympathy, their almost xenophobic rejection of the photographers highlights their insularity, although they themselves are – like Bernard's family and much of the community – Polish immigrants. However, as Joël Magny points out, the photographers represent a milieu so far removed from the family's experience that it is perceived as a fantasy land, which also partly explains the almost dream-like way the sequence opens (Magny 1992: 90).

The concluding sections of the film focus alternately on characters who stay and those who leave. Philippe and Elisabeth will return after a two-month absence to find Agnès working as a cashier, already unhappy in her marriage. She seriously regrets not going on with school as she tells Bernard after a quarrel with Rocky. Then in what becomes a leitmotiv in Pialat's treatment of couples, she confides that she has always loved him, that 'C'est mal foutu la vie, on ne peut jamais aimer ceux qu'on aime vraiment' ('Life is all screwed up, you can never love the people you really love').

Elisabeth, like Agnès, will 'stay', although not, perhaps, in school. We next see her, pregnant, sitting in the opening lecture of her philosophy class. Here the film loops back to the beginning as we hear the same lecture that the professor gave Elisabeth's class the year before. Her apparent disgust that she will have to listen to the same things all over again make it unlikely that she will pass her exams and graduate. Bernard and Patrick take off for Paris in a van marked Lens that Patrick – to Bernard's amusement – has trouble getting into gear. Patrick's family waves them off as his father, gesticulating with some urgency as the van lurches forward, tries to guide them safely out into the street. The sequence functions emblematically, providing a visible equivalent of the father's goodwill – and the boys' inexperience. The final shots bring us back to Elisabeth's family, as her mother is shown curling a ribbon to put in one of several elaborate table arrangements suitable for a wedding. 'A quoi tu rêves ma fille' ('what are you dreaming about'), she says affectionately to her daughter, seated across the room. 'A rien' ('Nothing'), Elisabeth replies, rising and going over to her mother, kissing her cheek and resting her head on her mother's shoulder. It is her mother who has the last word in the film, as she looks with satisfaction at her handiwork: 'je crois que tout le monde sera content' ('I think that everyone will be pleased').

The juxtaposition of sequences that focus alternatively on those who leave and those who stay, when it is clear that they might have – without doing violence to the logic of the narrative – been presented in reverse order, tends to cancel out the difference. Within the universe of the film everyone who leaves Lens comes back, and while Patrick has tentatively lined up a job in a bank in Paris, Bernard has no real plans. The two can afford to drift only until October when they will no longer get unemployment benefit. Elisabeth's mindless reverie as her mother prepares for her wedding suggests that she is also, in her own way, drifting, although her attachment to Philippe may prove stronger than that of Agnès to Rocky. Ultimately, despite the sweetness of Elisabeth's mother's tone, her final words can only be taken literally for the brief interval of the final shot. Within the larger context of the film they seem at best ambiguous; their apparent optimism giving way to irony.

Style and form

One of the most striking qualities of *Passe ton bac d'abord* is that it lacks a driving narrative line; there is no gradual development of a given situation to a dramatic – or comic – climax. The characters appear, disappear and reappear somewhat unpredictably from sequence to sequence, there is rarely a logical or narrative necessity for their presence – a case in point being the sequence when the proprietor of the local café turns up at the beach town where the group of friends has gone camping, or the sudden reappearance of Philippe and Elisabeth near the end of the film. Nor in fact do the sequences succeed one another according to a particular logic. The sequence in which Patrick argues with his sister about the relative value of Bob Marley's music as they walk along the beach has no clear dramatic function and the brief rendez-vous between the cynical brunette and the café owner might have figured in a number of different places in the film. In this sense there is a certain narrative aimlessness that reflects the young protagonists' own lack of direction, but which also corresponds formally to the existential question – reiterated in various forms throughout the film – 'Qu'est-ce que tu vas faire?' ('What are you going to do?').

The loop created by Pialat's reprise of the philosophy professor's introductory lecture suggests that the younger generation will inevitably repeat the pattern of their parents' lives, the loop functioning as a figure of entrapment. Yet Pialat was unhappy with the circular effect, claiming it was too pat, too clichéd, but that it remained 'faute de mieux' given the financial difficulties of the project (Pialat 1979: 46). He does attenuate the circularity by appending the final scene between Elisabeth and her mother. This allows the film to conclude on a moment of quiet intimacy, although it is impossible to distinguish Elisabeth's apparent serenity from resignation. Pialat claimed that he did not consider the film pessimistic – and certainly it is the only one of his films that deliberately reaches for comic effects. Its extraordinary focus on banal moments: buying postcards, eating candy and pastries at the beach and its mosaic of desultory conversations and chance encounters provided a new model to replace more traditional dramatic structures. The film did surprisingly well, restoring Pialat's confidence and attracting a younger audience to his work. It is now shown more frequently on television and is perhaps the most well known of his films of the 1970s. This success allowed him to move on, but also to return to making films that grew out of his own personal experience.

References

Chevassu, François (1990), 'Les Drôles de chemins de Maurice Pialat', *Revue du cinéma*, no. 466.

Kermabon, Jacques (1983), '*A nos amours*: Pialat, un peintre du vide', *Revue du cinéma*, no. 389.

Magny, Joël (1992), *Maurice Pialat*, Paris, Cahiers du cinéma.

Mérigeau, Pascal (2002), *Pialat*, Paris, Editions Grasset et Fasquelle.

Pialat, Maurice (1973), *Nous ne vieillirons pas ensemble* in *Avant-scène du cinéma*, no. 134.

Pialat, Maurice (1974), 'Trois Rencontres avec Maurice Pialat', *Positif*, no. 159.

Pialat, Maurice (1979), 'Entretien', *Cinéma 72*, no. 250.

Pialat, Maurice (1979b), 'Entretien', *Cahiers du cinéma*, no. 304.

Pialat, Maurice (1980), 'Entretien', *Cinématographe*, no. 57.

Pialat, Maurice (1980b), 'Entretien', *Positif*, no. 235.

Pialat, Maurice (1984), *A nos amours: scénario et dialogue du film*, Paris, L'Herminier.

Vernet, Marc (1991), 'Pathos de travelling arrière', *Vertigo: rhétoriques du cinéma*, nos. 6–7.

Vincendeau, Ginette (1990), 'Therapeutic realism: Maurice Pialat's *A nos amours*' in Vincendeau and Hayward (eds), *French Film: Texts and Contexts*, London/New York, Routledge.

5

Family portraits II: *Loulou*, *A nos amours* and *Police*

Loulou

Although Pialat began work on *Loulou* almost immediately after finishing *Passe ton bac d'abord*, the real events that inspired it took place almost ten years earlier. The scenario for *Loulou*, written by Arlette Langmann, was based on the break-up of her relationship with Pialat over her affair with 'Dédé', who had been involved in the production of *La Maison des bois*. Langmann kept only the kernel of the story, fictionalising the circumstances of the relationship while attempting to convey its emotional intensity. Langmann's central character, Nelly, played by Isabelle Huppert, abandons her husband of three years, André, an art-loving publicist (Guy Marchand), and her bourgeois family, for Louis, known as Loulou (Gérard Depardieu), a young tough character with a prison record whom she encounters at a nightclub.

As in all of Pialat's films, the casting represented a crucial 'fleshing out' of the story. The choice of Depardieu – rather than the lanky, more sardonic Jacques Dutronc, whom Pialat had initially considered for the role of Loulou – and Isabelle Huppert – rather than Miou Miou or Sylvia Kristel – inevitably had important repercussions. Depardieu, in his late twenties, beginning to emerge as a major actor after the success of Blier's 1974 film *Les Valseuses* in which he also played a 'loubard' (a young tough, living on the margins) brought both his image in Blier's film and his earlier reputation as a teen delinquent to his portrayal of Loulou. His lank blond hair and unwashed, unshaven look; his heavier, more powerful physique become a foil for the dark, lanky, balding figure of Guy Marchand. In addition, the contrast between André's well-cut suits and Loulou's heavy black leather jacket with its many zippers provides a visual shorthand for their wearer's class and cultural differences. 'T'as vu sa gueule?' says the incredulous André to Nelly after meeting Loulou in a café, 'tu peux pas rester avec ce mec-là' ('Take a look at his face ... You can't stay with this guy').

The filming did not go smoothly and the heavy atmosphere on the set reflected both Pialat's uncertainties about the project and his actors' discontents. Both Marchand and Depardieu resented Pialat's frequent absences, his apparent inability to decide what he wanted, his constant needling and criticism of their work. When the filming was over Depardieu gave an interview in which he declared that the only thing that could persuade him to work with Pialat again would be the money.

> C'est très difficile de travailler dans la merde. Tout est noir, tout est dégueulasse, tout est pourri, tout est vendu! Travaillez là-dedans demande de la santé et je pense que son histoire qu'il a eue avec Jean Yanne n'est pas un hasard [...] Moi, j'ai décidé de m'en foutre et de l'enfoncer un peu plus, et de lui dire: tout ça c'est de la merde ce qu'on fait.[1] (Gonzalez 1985: 146)

Disgusted, Depardieu refused to see the final film. Two years later, it came as a revelation: 'à la projection j'ai tout compris' (Depardieu 1988: 77–8) ('when I saw the film, I understood everything'), he admitted. By contrast, Isabelle Huppert claimed that she knew the work was going well, and considered the atmosphere on the set a crucial factor in Pialat's obtaining certain effects: 'C'est grâce à ça, ou à cause de ça, que Loulou a cette ambiance moite, trouble, physique, fantastique!'[2] (Magny 1992: 30).

Narrative and characterisation

Loulou opens as two different couples' relationships unravel. The slightly hungover Loulou is not fully awake when his brother Rémy

1 'It is really hard to work in shit. Everything is depressing, everything is disgusting, everything is rotten, everything is corrupt. To work in that atmosphere requires a healthy attitude and I think that the quarrel he had with Jean Yanne wasn't just a coincidence [...] I decided I didn't care and that I would try to rub it in a little and tell him that what we were doing was just crap.'
2 'It's thanks to [the atmosphere on the set] or because of it that *Loulou* has that clammy, murky, physical, fantastic quality!'

slams the door on Dominique, Loulou's neglected girlfriend, telling her to get lost. When Loulou later finds her crying, he tries to placate her with kisses and an offer to take her dancing. The next sequence opens as André walks around among the dancers at a nightclub looking for someone. Visibly out of sorts, he settles himself just off the dance floor to wait. A point of view shot shows that he has spied Nelly, who is dancing with Loulou. Loulou, clearly drunk, is hanging all over her, while she smiles half-embarrassedly and dodges his kisses. She disengages herself when she sees André, ultimately abandoning Loulou on the dance floor to join him. André berates her for the way she wiggles her behind as she dances and accuses her of wanting to sleep with Loulou. Although Nelly dismisses his accusations with an exasperated 'ah arrête' ('oh stop'), André will not let the subject drop. Furious, Nelly stalks off, but André follows and slaps her in the face. Despite the intervention of Nelly's sister-in-law Annie (played by Arlette Langmann – the casting has its ironies) who attempts to smooth things over, Nelly refuses to leave with André. Her impulsive decision to stay and dance results in her spending the night with Loulou and in a violent quarrel with André that effectively ends their marriage.

These opening sequences are particularly disorienting because Pialat makes no attempt to situate the action – or even identify the characters, beyond conveying the fact that Nelly and André are married. Langmann's character emerges out of nowhere and Pialat does not establish the nature of her relationship to the couple until the following sequence. Moreover, both sequences take place in dimly or unevenly lit, sometimes crowded, spaces. What is clear, however, is the intensity of the attraction between Loulou and Nelly, conveyed almost entirely by their movements and physical presence. Loulou gravitates toward Nelly, frequently attempting to pull or bring her closer if she shows signs of moving away. In the last frames of the nightclub sequence he cuts in between Nelly and her sister-in-law twice, effectively blocking the latter's effort to remonstrate with her to leave. He then draws Nelly back into his arms, rubbing his face against hers as she puts her arm around him. Their embrace on the dance floor merely anticipates the next shot of the two of them in bed.

Just as in the case of André and Loulou, the contrast between Nelly and Loulou, their clothing, manner and tastes are visible signs of the class differences that separate them. Nelly, a gold ring on her little finger, looks 'classy', so much so that Loulou formally asks André for permission to dance with her. He cannot carry off the gesture, hesitating, groping for words and backing away awkwardly when she responds that she is tired. Later, when they make love, she will be disconcerted by his tattoos. If they both smoke, it is not the same brand of cigarettes (although she will share one of his) and he will make a face at the smell of the cognac she drinks, not even interested in tasting it. Pialat never attempts any political or psychological analysis of the underlying causes of these differences in behaviour and taste; the couple embodies them as visible signs of internalised value systems.

True to her assertion to Dominique that she will take Loulou just as he is, Nelly even takes financial responsibility for him, paying their hotel bills and later their rent. Loulou does not hesitate to dole out some of her money to his mother. Although André accuses her of buying a man, Nelly retorts that it is normal for her to pay as Loulou has no job. Nelly also assumes considerable risk on Loulou's account, accompanying him – if initially under protest – as he and a friend rob a store, then helps them unload their haul. When Loulou invites Lulu – just out of jail and with nowhere to go – to stay in their small apartment, she does not protest. If on two stressful occasions she turns to André, she ultimately dashes his hope of re-establishing their relationship on its old footing by announcing that she is pregnant with Loulou's child. Near the end of the film, when she and Loulou have lunch with his mother, she completely abandons her under-stated elegance to wear a black leather jacket over a blood-red blouse and matching polka-dot skirt, the change in style a visible sign of her desire to fit into his milieu. However, her pregnancy and André's refusal to support Loulou, albeit indirectly, by continuing to employ her, create a situation in which her values and expectations clash with Loulou's. Both feel betrayed when Nelly decides she must have an abortion.

While Nelly's apparently sudden decisions, first to leave André, and then later to have an abortion, drive the film, Pialat's reworking of Langmann's scenario displaces her character from the centre of the narrative. He introduces Nelly after both Loulou and André so that she is seen in relation to them as part of a traditional romantic triangle. The gender displacement objectifies her as the desired woman, leaving her motivations obscure to the viewer and puzzling and painful subjects of speculation for both André and Loulou. Loulou emerges as the centre of the filmic narrative by default. Ironically he becomes the only non-bourgeois with whom Pialat can identify, but also represents Pialat's real-life rival. Pialat's negative feelings toward this character played out in a sequence actually filmed but ultimately eliminated, in which Loulou was murdered (Pialat 1980b: 28). In the finished film Pialat overcomes his ambivalence by creating a *rapprochement* between the husband and the lover. After initially setting up a stereotyped contrast between Loulou as the virile, but uncultured and inarticulate lowlife, and André as the articulate and cultivated, but more sexually repressed and conflicted bourgeois, Pialat then moves to undercut it. He gives each a 'double' who distracts from their differences and allows them to meet on common ground.

The first of the two doubles, a stand-in for André, is Nelly's very proper bourgeois brother Michel, who figures only in a single sequence. It is arguably Pialat's closest approach to social satire, and Michel represents a recurrent figure in Pialat's cinema, the odious bourgeois. Here, the not yet brother-in-law has been invited to lunch. He arrives in a chauffeured car – seemingly from some government ministry – making an entrance similar to that of the Parisian photographers in *Passe ton bac d'abord*. While the lunch is ostensibly a social occasion, Pialat avoids any shots in which the three are shown eating together. Instead he cuts to the final minutes of the visit in which Michel gets to the point, quizzing Loulou patronisingly about his prospects for work now that he is about to become a father. When Loulou makes it clear that he has no particular skills, but also no interest in low-wage manual labour, Michel condescendingly offers to set him up in a café or some other small business. The arrival of Loulou's adopted brother Pierrot, who invites Loulou and Nelly to join the family for lunch on Sunday, puts an end to the strained conversation and precipitates Michel's exit.

The second of these doubles, a double of Loulou, is his friend Lulu, the consonance of their names suggesting their similarity. Both live on the margins, both have spent time in prison. Taller than Loulou, more traditionally handsome, more articulate, Lulu might have taken Loulou's place as the romantic lead if it were not for his handicap, a paralysed arm. More mature than Loulou, he seems equally drawn to Nelly, buying her flowers, then offering to help her in the kitchen. After the lunch at Loulou's mother's, the camera will linger on him as he dances a slow dance with Nelly, providing a counterpoint to the nightclub scenes of her dancing with Loulou. This secondary 'rivalry' and Lulu's very courtly manner toward Nelly reflect negatively both on Loulou and on André who, like Jean in *Nous ne vieillirons pas ensemble*, is alternately abusive and needy, expecting his wife to mother him. In contrast to the sexual attraction that draws Nelly to Loulou, André's more bourgeois relationship with Nelly grows out of a shared work life in which personal and financial interests are inseparable. In fact, André only succeeds in re-establishing some intimacy with Nelly after she leaves him for Loulou by continuing their work relationship. After Nelly's departure André remains a solitary figure who fades into the background, reappearing in the final sequence in response to Loulou's appeal.

By contrast, Loulou is rarely seen alone and never for long. He is surrounded by an extended family including his mother, brother Rémy, married sister Marie Jo, her husband Thomas and their two small children, his 'adopted' brother Pierrot, friends from the *banlieue* and from prison, as well as the regulars of the local café – whose owner, René, takes up a collection every time one of his patrons goes to jail. Associated with a community, Loulou has no place of his own, sleeping at his brother's, or staying in a hotel and borrowed apartments with Nelly, until she (a bourgeoise more attached to private property) rents an apartment for the two of them. Loulou calls Nelly his fiancée, but seems uncertain whether he can sustain an exclusive relationship with her – confessing to her with some anguish that he might be tempted by Dominique if the occasion presented itself. He is no less insecure about his relationship with Nelly than André, confiding to his brother in a rare moment of introspection that women are really only interested in him for sex. His apparent willingness to allow one of René's clients to proposition Nelly might be interpreted as a test of her more exclusive personal interest in him. Unsure of himself and unsure of Nelly, Loulou shows no inclination to withdraw into what André refers to as their lovenest, inviting Lulu to share their space.

Loulou's sense of belonging to a family and community, to which he contributes when he can and which sustains him – although just at subsistence level – sets him apart from Nelly and André (and by extension their class) for whom money serves as a guarantee of security and independence. Loulou appears to have sufficient confidence in his place within the family and larger family/community to believe, as he movingly tells Nelly's brother, that his child will never go without enough to eat. The warmth and openness of this family/ community – in which there is always enough to feed a hungry child, and always a place for one more person at the table – is celebrated in the sequence of the sunny Sunday picnic at Loulou's mother's.

The picnic sequence, discussed in greater detail in the next section, marks a turning point in the film. The festive atmosphere and congeniality recall the wedding reception in *L'Enfance nue*. Both are expansive moments in which everyone, adopted child or homeless ex-con, finds love and acceptance. Yet there are early signs of trouble in the black mood of Marie Jo's husband Thomas, who refuses to let his family join the meal. His seething jealousy and hostility boil over when he turns on Lulu and Pierrot brandishing a shotgun, claiming they are flirting with his wife. Loulou and Rémy finally wrest the gun away from him but not before he fires several times. Just as they have subdued him, he breaks away and savagely attacks Pierrot. When it is all over, Loulou looks visibly shaken, apologising to Nelly as he stammers 'j'y peux rien' ('I can't do anything about it'). To avoid further violence, Pierrot leaves with them; Nelly takes his arm as they walk towards the car, Loulou at her side. The sequence recapitulates the dynamics of *L'Enfance nue*: the drama of inclusion/exclusion, acceptance/rejection that makes 'flight' or 'expulsion' (from the couple, family or community) one of the most persistent motifs of Pialat's films.

By the end of this sequence the existence of a welcoming and nourishing working-class community appears to be a nostalgic or utopian illusion, undercut by darker realities. The family is in a precarious position, supported primarily by Loulou's mother, who works as a cleaning lady in the city and indirectly by Nelly, who has been fired by André. Of the men, only Pierrot has a job. Loulou, who by his own admission, takes things as they come, expresses only vague ideas about looking for work after his child is born, and only when prodded by Pierrot and his mother. In contrast to Nelly and André, he does not associate work (or the money it earns) with independence, personal satisfaction or the possibility for self-expression. Earlier, when Nelly's brother asked him, all practical considerations aside, what sort of work he preferred, he replies 'rien' ('nothing'). Ultimately the only 'job' he undertakes in the film is a robbery. His apparent guilelessness and freewheeling behaviour are part of his charm, but also vulnerabilities. This is brought home in an earlier sequence when he is attacked and stabbed after jostling a woman in a crowded bar. The violence takes him completely off-guard. He remains equally oblivious to the potential for violence within his own family, although it strikes at the heart of his community.

The apparent disjunction between the picnic and the very brief, almost flat and colourless sequence that follows it is one of the most disorienting in the film. Nelly, dressed in a shapeless white top, clearing her throat to find her voice, begins speaking on a public telephone. Nothing in the shot provides a clue to help to situate the action. However, when she says that it is over and that she woke up an hour ago, it becomes clear that she has had an abortion. Nothing overtly links this sequence to the previous one, yet their juxtaposition suggests that Thomas's actions played a part in Nelly's decision and the abortion represents a visceral rejection of Loulou's potentially violent and unstable milieu.

On Nelly's return after the abortion, Loulou remarks bitterly that her family must be happy and reproaches her for letting him hope for a child. She replies that they could not have kept a child as they were barely managing. When he insists that he would have found work after the baby came, she expresses doubt. 'Fallait me faire confiance' ('You should have trusted me') he replies. Pialat subsequently regretted not concluding the film with this scene (Pialat 1980b: 24). In fact, the subsequent scenes weaken the dramatic value of this exchange by suggesting, with a twist worthy of Rohmer, that the couple might have a future.

After leaving Nelly to rest in their apartment, Loulou meets André as he emerges from the Metro, their brief exchange making it clear that Loulou appealed to his rival to help him to understand his relationship with Nelly. The two men move off together down the street although the viewer never hears their exchange. In the concluding scene, Loulou reappears, alone, and very drunk. He finds Nelly in René's bar, kisses her and the two of them stumble off together. While the film ends ambiguously, there is little chance either André or Loulou will soon become fathers, although they have established a form of masculine brotherhood. Moreover, André's observation to Nelly earlier in the film that all of the couples they know are breaking up seems no less true for Loulou's milieu – where Thomas's violent jealousy has alienated his wife and divided the family.

Style and form

Pialat wryly referred to *Loulou* as 'a film between two doors' ('un film entre deux portes') because of the 'incalculable' number of scenes that began or ended with the opening or closing of a door (Pialat 1980: 4). It is also a film caught between two different formal approaches: the emphasis on long takes, characteristic of *La Gueule ouverte* or *Nous ne vieillirons pas ensemble*, versus the more fragmented 'chronicle' adopted for *Passe ton bac d'abord*. Pialat wanted to move towards a greater emphasis on editing, which he associated with greater technical skill and professionalism. As he told an interviewer at *Positif*: 'ayant commencé à faire des films sur le tard, en me débrouillant avec les moyens à bord, en bricolant, j'ai fait des films vaille que vaille et puis, un jour, j'ai réalisé qu'il fallait devenir professionnel et passer à autre chose'.[3] Yet he remained ambivalent about 'well-constructed' films, reflecting in the same interview that: 'c'est vrai aussi peut-être, que dans ces films mieux faits on ne trouvera pas ces petits moments de grâce qu'il y a dans les films mal foutus'[4] (Pialat 1980b: 24).

Loulou's composition reflects Pialat's ambivalence, while the finished film proves that he was not seeking formal perfection in any conventional sense. The nocturnal images are frequently dark and murky, to the point where during the robbery it is difficult to tell what is going on. The dialogue is frequently unintelligible, although the fact that it is often banal, repetitious and even frequently crude is clearly intended to reflect both a milieu and 'real' conversation. Pialat does not cut moments when actors flub their lines or amateurs miss cues and speak out of turn – a notable example being the woman in René's café, eager to pay her bill, who cuts off Depardieu in the middle of a sentence, forcing him to start over again. Causal and temporal relationships between certain sequences are frequently unclear and the construction of the film is by no means conventionally dramatic. Crucial events are elided (Nelly's abortion); potential dramatic high points (the robbery and the fight in which Loulou is knifed) are flattened out because the viewer cannot fully follow the action. The

3 'having started making films rather late, making do with whatever means were available, improvising, I've made films that are worth what they're worth but then, one day, I realised that you had to become more professional and move on to other things'.

4 'it's also true perhaps that in these well-made films you don't find the little moments of grace that are in films that are thrown together'.

street fight, a nocturnal sequence like the robbery, is filmed in a fluid long shot with a handheld camera. In the mêlée, it is difficult to distinguish what is going on, only the click of a switchblade, clearly audible over the sounds of the scuffle, alerts the viewer to the coming violence.

Pialat does not so much compose a story as involve the viewer as a witness in the events as they unfold, even if they take an unexpected turn. 'Le réalisme, c'est quand même filmer la scène que nous sommes en train de vivre' ('Realism, after all, is filming the scene that we are in the act of living'), he told interviewers when *Loulou* came out (Pialat 1980b: 27). In *Loulou,* this meant continuing to film when the bed frame broke under Depardieu's weight in the first love scene between Loulou and Nelly – or including the elderly lady who apparently barges into the film to take Loulou and André to task for fighting in the courtyard of her apartment building. She follows them out into the street demanding that someone pay for the damage to the mailboxes. Her presence, like the crash of the bed, creates a diversion, inflects the scene by injecting a comic note and forces the actors to respond spontaneously to new material.

The Sunday at Loulou's mother's represents a crucial example of Pialat's constant willingness to reimagine and reinvent the narrative structure of his film. The sequence runs slightly more than fifteen minutes from the time that Loulou's mother hears the gates close behind her guests and turns to welcome them, until the moment when Nelly and Loulou escort Pierrot back to their car. While the sequence marks a turning point in the finished film, this could not have been established prior to the actual filming, which was only authorised at the last minute.

Formally, the sequence reconciles Pialat's initial tendency to film in long takes with his greater use of cuts. During the first part of the sequence when the guests arrive, mill about and settle at the table, supple camera movements track the actors as they move. The first cut comes only some two minutes into the action and later cuts are minimal and unobtrusive. Nelly, seated next to Loulou's mother, is at the centre of the visual field, tightly framed by the guests crowded around the table, while Loulou sits across the table from her. Despite her gaiety and her appetite, almost everything is too strong for Nelly: first she chokes on the aperitif, then on the vinaigrette for the oysters, which sends her into a coughing fit. While purely anecdotal, Nelly's reaction takes on greater symbolic importance as the sequence unfolds. It is her mood change, associated with Loulou's apparent lack of interest in finding work, that first signals the darkening of the afternoon. Loulou, noticing that she has become abstracted, reaches across the table to her, but although she kisses his fingers, she no longer appears fully engaged. The more violent shift in the sequence is announced by the dog's sudden attack on a hen. Then, when Thomas emerges, shotgun in hand, the rhythm of the sequence accelerates in a series of quick cuts between him and the others who try in vain to reason with him. The editing of the struggle increases the sense of drama and confusion. Only as order is re-established will there be a return to longer shots. The sequence is in many ways a *tour de force*, standing out initially as bright and sunny against the many darker nocturnal scenes in the film. As a group portrait, it has a signature – Loulou's apparently offhand answer to his niece's question about one of her toys: 'Comment il s'appelle?' ('What is his name?'), is 'Maurice'.

The film was chosen as one of three French entries at Cannes in 1980, but won no awards. When *Loulou* finally reached theatres in September, it failed to measure up to the popular success of *Nous ne vieillirons pas ensemble*. The most successful films that year were more accessible, among them the teen-party film *La Boum*, Sophie Marceau's film debut (Mérigeau 2002: 186–7). However, *Loulou* brought Pialat an important connection, Isabelle Huppert's partner, Daniel Toscan du Plantier, then at Gaumont, who played an important role in Pialat's next two films. 'The Toscan years' brought Pialat greater public recognition and a Palme d'or.

A nos amours

A nos amours marks both an end and a beginning for Pialat. A key film in his career, it is arguably his greatest film, a popular and critical success that finally brought him the status of a major director. It represents the culmination of his autobiographical films and an artistic profession of faith. It is also the last film that he would make with Arlette Langmann.

Like *Passe ton bac d'abord*, *A nos amours* began as an adaptation of Arlette Langmann's autobiographical scenario *Les Filles du faubourg*. Pialat and Langmann returned to the original scenario, focusing on

Langmann's character, 'Suzanne', rather than the more complicated interactions of the six friends in her original story. To simplify filming exterior shots and cut costs, they abandoned the idea of setting the events in the 1960s. The most fateful decision, however, would be to give the role of Suzanne to a fifteen-year-old girl named Sandrine Bonnaire, who had appeared in response to an ad for the casting of *Les Meurtrières*. Bonnaire's energy, her charisma, her gift for improvisation and responsiveness to the emotional climate of a scene overcame any hesitations about casting her for the part of Suzanne. Her presence gave the film greater credibility as a 1980s film, and resulted in another, apparently minor, but ultimately crucial decision. Pialat opted to play Suzanne's father, claiming (like Renoir when he stepped into the role of Octave in *The Rules of the Game*) that he could not find anyone else to play the part (Bergala 1983: 12).

Like *La Gueule ouverte*, more than half of *A nos amours* was filmed in a single décor, a large apartment just off the Place Victor Hugo. Arlette Langmann recalled the huge rooms – the windows masked to make the space appear more modest – which gave Pialat many of the advantages of filming in a studio coupled with the authenticity of location shooting (Pialat 1984: 139). Nonetheless the work advanced slowly and at the end of February, having exhausted the available funds, he was forced stop work on the film. It would be June before he could resume filming for another four weeks, part of the time in Hyères. It is these scenes, suffused with Mediterranean light, that open the film.

Narrative and characterisation

A nos amours begins in a summer camp for girls on the Mediterranean as the sixteen-year-old Suzanne rehearses for a leading role in their amateur production of de Musset's romantic tragedy *On ne badine pas avec l'amour*. She then slips away to see her boyfriend Luc, who is camping in the area, but quarrels with him. Later, she lets herself be seduced by an American she meets in a bar at the port, quickly regretting her impulsiveness and fearing Luc's reaction.

The action then shifts to the Paris apartment/workshop where she lives with her parents, who are artisans working in the fur trade. Although her older brother Robert works in the family business, he aspires to be a writer and is involved in the theatre, his artistic aspirations encouraged by their father, who compares his work to that of Marcel Pagnol. A series of sequences stretching over weeks, or months, show Suzanne's break-up with Luc and her parents' wrangling. They are often at odds with each other over Suzanne's behaviour and her relationships with boys. One night after her father waits up for her, he and Suzanne exchange confidences and he tells her what he has not yet told anyone else, that he is moving out. It is never clear whether he is leaving his wife for another woman, as he dodges Suzanne's questions and disappears from the film until the penultimate sequence. After his departure, Suzanne becomes involved with a succession of lovers, although she has not forgotten Luc. Meanwhile there are repeated and violent family scenes in which Suzanne's mother, overworked and depressed, becomes hysterical and attacks Suzanne verbally and physically. Robert, very attached to his mother and disgusted by Suzanne's promiscuity, also attacks and slaps her. Ultimately Suzanne asks Robert to put her in boarding school, discovering later on one of her weekends in the city that Luc has become her best friend's boyfriend.

A new lover, Jean-Pierre, provides greater stability for her, but just before their wedding Luc calls and asks her to meet him. He insists that he has always loved her and urges her to come back to him. Although she hesitates, she tells him that it is impossible. Six months later, during a family reception, it becomes clear that Robert has had some literary success and married the sister of an eminent critic, perhaps in the hope of advancing his career. As the family gathers at the diningroom table, the tension between Jean-Pierre and Jacques (Robert's brother-in-law the critic) takes the form of a sharp exchange about the merits of Picasso's art. However, all conversation abruptly ceases as the father barges in, apparently expecting to show the apartment to a prospective tenant. He brazenly sits down at the table with his family and their guests, helping himself to dessert. As they sit in stunned silence, he attacks Jacques for publishing an article highly critical of Robert's work in his literary review, then accuses Robert of selling out to the establishment – ruefully noting the power of money. Finally, rephrasing a remark attributed to Van Gogh :'la tristesse durera toujours' ('the sadness will last forever'), he insults the entire group. 'C'est vous qui êtes tristes' ('You are the sad ones') he claims, singling out Suzanne to ask if she is on his side. Finally, Betty, furious, puts an end to the scene by slapping him, then shoving him towards the door.

In the final sequence, apparently some months later, Suzanne says goodbye to her father, having come to tell him that she is leaving for California with Michel, one of her brother's friends. As they talk on the bus to the airport, he chides her for leaving her husband and for expecting others to love her without loving in return. Yet he is also warm and affectionate, enthusiastic about her trip to San Diego, claiming he and Betty had once thought of going to Canada. He has heard that in San Diego it is possible to see schools of whales just offshore. 'Tu dois rester là-bas', he tells her. 'Ça te ferait du bien, t'as qu'à ne pas revenir. J'irai te voir de temps en temps. Je n'suis pas encore fini'.[5] When he leaves her at the airport, the camera follows him until his bus heads into a tunnel, then the film cuts back to Suzanne in the plane. A final medium close-up shows her looking out the aircraft window, her expression uncertain.

On its release, *A nos amours* was saluted as the most developed and finished of Pialat's films, a complex reworking of characters, issues and themes that had preoccupied him in earlier films. Alain Bergala, writing for *Cahiers du cinéma*, claimed that among the filmmakers whose work 'counted' Pialat had become 'celui dont les films couvrent le champ le plus large et le plus hétérogène de la réalité française contemporaine'[6] (Bergala 1983: 8). In fact, *A nos amours* condenses what might have been several rather different films into a single complex filmic narrative focused on the relationship between Suzanne and her father. These alternative narrative possibilities subsist in the final film, if only in latent or fragmentary form, complicating and enriching it. The most obvious of these is Langmann's story, part autobiography, part social document, about a girl growing up in the 1960s who must deal with the death of her father (a narrative that might have led Pialat to rework elements from *Passe ton bac d'abord* and *La Gueule ouverte*). However, the film also contains elements of a contemporary reworking of de Musset's romantic tragedy *On ne badine pas avec l'amour*, and two different documentaries. The first of these might have been a film about the making of *A nos amours*,

---

5 'You should stay there, it would do you good. All you have to do is not come back. I'll visit you now and then. I'm not all washed up yet.'

6 'the one whose films cover the widest and most heterogeneous area of contemporary French reality'.

focusing on the director's doubts about his art, his conflicts with his actors and disillusionment with the film industry. The second would have focused more narrowly on the collaboration between a fifty-eight year-old film director and the extraordinarily talented fifteen year-old he discovered and cast as his daughter in a quasi-autobiographical film. In some cases these latent narratives call attention to themselves through internal inconsistencies or formal disjunctions – as Pascal Bonitzer suggests when he notes the contrast between the sunny opening scenes and the rest of the film, set in more sombre and confining family or urban spaces: 'Il semble qu'il y ait dans *A nos amours* ... comme la trace mal effacée d'un autre film ... dont le récit se serait passé au soleil, au bord de la Méditerrannée entre des adolescents jouant *On ne badine pas avec l'amour*. De ce film il reste peu de chose'[7] (Bonitzer 1983: 6).

Langmann maintained that Pialat remained faithful to her story, although she regretted the lack of precision in the relationship between the mother and daughter (Mérigeau 2002: 226). Yet the substitution of Sandrine Bonnaire for Langmann, anchoring the film in the 1980s, results in a rather different kind of social document. The family's Polish-Jewish origins and the nature of their work are only briefly evoked, and remain undeveloped. If the 1960s still 'haunt the film', as Ginette Vincendeau indicates, it is primarily in the parents' (particularly the mother's) attitude toward Suzanne's sexuality. If Suzanne's father is willing to imagine (perhaps more incestuously than permissively) his daughter with a lover, her mother holds to the belief that a girl should remain a virgin until she is married. The clash between the 1960s and the 1980s sparks the violent disputes between Suzanne, her mother and her brother. Moreover, viewed in the context of the 1980s, Betty's hysteria as well as her deep depression and apparent despair at the break-up of her marriage seem morbidly excessive, more understandable if she were reacting to her husband's death. The temporal shift also supports Pialat's decision during the shooting to have the father walk out on his wife and family. At a time when there was less social and moral pressure on the father to remain a part of the family circle, Pialat could create the sense of loss and betrayal that

7 'There seem to be still visible traces in *A nos amours* ... of another film, ... one where the story would have taken place on the Mediterranean involving adolescents playing parts in [Alfred de Musset's tragic drama] *On ne badine pas avec l'amour*. Little remains of this film.'

had profoundly affected Langmann without portraying her father's death.

Most crucial in the reworking of Langmann's story, however, was its conflation with Pialat's own autobiographical narrative, unwritten but embodied in the characters, situations and themes of his earlier films. *Les Filles du faubourg* provided the advantage of a story that Pialat could appropriate without completely reworking it – as he had been forced to do in *La Gueule ouverte*. The principal characters in Langmann's scenario were familiar figures in both his personal and professional life. His intense, if stormy friendship with her brother, his professional ties to her brother-in-law Jean-Pierre Rassam and his ongoing relationship (and artistic collaboration) with Langmann herself were important to his own story.

The choice of Evelyne Ker, as Suzanne's mother, suggests an effort to recreate some semblance of this personal and professional universe in the film. Not only had Ker been the eponymous heroine in Pialat's first fictional short, *Janine*, but she knew the Langmann family. Another professional connection, Dominique Besnehard, a highly successful casting director who had had his differences with Pialat during the filming of *Passe ton bac d'abord*, was persuaded to put his other professional projects on hold in order to accept the role of Suzanne's brother, Claude Berri's role. Jacques Fieschi, then editor of an important film journal, *Cinématographe*, was invited to play the role of the 'brother-in-law', standing in for the film producer Jean-Pierre Rassam. Fieschi's connections to the film industry and to Pialat himself – whom he had featured in his review on more than one occasion – also figured importantly in Pialat's asking him to play what amounted to a small walk-on part in the film.

Only Sandrine Bonnaire, the talented amateur, had no personal connection to either the family drama or the professional world that came together in the film. However, as Alain Philippon suggests, the subject of *A nos amours* is no less a story about the cinematic couple formed by Pialat and Bonnaire, their extraordinary collaboration marked by a singular intimacy and complicity – but also by troubling overtones of seduction (Philippon 1983: 19). The ambiguity of the very first (pre-credit) image in the film underscores Bonnaire's youth and her lack of experience. It is a medium close-up of an adolescent girl in a striped T-shirt, sitting at a table, alternately consulting a text and speaking haltingly to the camera – as though to an invisible partner –

as she tries to learn her lines. The viewer's initial impression of a documentary image is subsequently integrated into the fictional narrative as the next shot shows Bonnaire/Suzanne repeating the same lines in the dress rehearsal for *On ne badine pas avec l'amour*. For viewers acquainted with Pialat's career or earlier films, the scene inevitably suggested the difficulties of working with young amateurs, as he had done in both *L'Enfance nue* and *Passe ton bac d'abord*.

Yet Pialat's pleasure in working with the extraordinary young actress he had discovered was tempered by the realisation that he would inevitably lose her as she went on to what promised to be a brilliant career. 'Je m'étais mis dans la tête que j'allais rester comme un vieux con à faire des films ringards et ... qu'on allait s'arracher Sandrine',[8] he confessed to Cyril Collard (Pialat 1984: 17). The fear of losing her filters into the narrative when, on the eve of her daughter's wedding, Betty reminisces about how Suzanne's father had adored his baby daughter, refusing to leave her alone for even a second because he was obsessed with the idea she would be kidnapped (a story the father will repeat in the final scene). Yet the father/director's desire to remain close to his 'daughter' is also at work in two crucial changes that Pialat introduced in the structure of Langmann's narrative. Refusing to 'die', he staged a surprise return during the penultimate scene, and wrote his own ending for the film – in which he and Bonnaire are alone together in a bus to the airport. The changes allow him to be more fully involved in the film but also lead him to compete with his daughter for the viewer's sympathy and attention.

Pialat's appropriation of Langmann's narrative results (as it did in *Loulou*) in a form of gender displacement. Ginette Vincendeau notes that Suzanne was originally the subject of a female narrative of self-exploration, but that in Pialat's film she becomes the object of directorial/spectatorial desire as well. The abrupt shift from the documentary feel of the rehearsal in the pre-credit sequence to the image of Suzanne during the credits makes this point clearly. Suzanne, dressed in pure white, stands alone, silhouetted against the blue of the Mediterranean like a goddess risen from the sea, as Klaus Nomi's sings Henry Purcell's *Cold Song*. As Vincendeau points out, this transformation reflects the focus on a beautiful, problematic, potentially

---

8 'I got it into my head that I was going to be left like an old fart making dated films and that ... people were going to fight over Sandrine.'

treacherous, young woman that is a classic motif of (male) auteur cinema. Yet the conflation of Pialat and Langmann's narratives also makes Suzanne a figure of cross-gender identification, she is 'both Langmann's heroine and Pialat's hero' (Vincendeau 1990: 259).

Pialat's identification with Suzanne emerges most clearly in the resemblance between father and daughter, both strong and independent figures who break away from the family. Pialat also emphasises an aspect of Suzanne's character that he sometimes ascribed to himself – an emotional 'coldness' that leads her to wonder if she has a 'dry heart' (Pialat 1980: 5; Pialat 1984: 13). Purcell's Cold Song is taken from 'The Frost Scene' in Dryden's King Arthur, in which Cupid attempts to waken the aged Frost Genius. The Frost Genius's plea – 'let me, let me, let me freeze, let me freeze again to death' – is associated with Suzanne in a curious juxtaposition of summer and winter, youth and age, sensuality and death. De Musset's tragedy then prefigures Suzanne's damaging trifling with love as well as both the failure of her relationship with Luc and her marriage.

The relationship with Luc merits greater attention than Suzanne's other liaisons, even her marriage, because she suspects that Luc may have been her greatest love. The cut between her last meeting with Luc and her pensive solitude at the beginning of the reception suggests that she remains emotionally attached to him even after her marriage. Her past happiness with Luc (like her relationship with her father) represents an intensity of emotion that has no outlet in sexual passion. In fact, her vision of the consummation of their love is the love-death of romantic narratives. 'J'étais tellement heureuse que j'avais l'impression de rêver. C'est pour ça que je voulais mourir avec toi sur la luge',[9] she tells him, remembering a time when they were together in Courchevel, in the Alps, when she was fifteen. If this snowy death connects thematically with the Cold Song, the romantic scenario they suggest breaks down. This is partly because Luc does not understand what Suzanne wants from him – anymore than Cyr Boitard, who played Luc, understood Pialat's dissatisfaction with his wooden acting style and monotone delivery (Pialat: 1983: 58) – but also because in the 1980s, unlike in de Musset's play, no one will die of love. What remains is Suzanne's suicidal urges, her 'marre de vivre'

9 'I was so happy that I thought I was dreaming. That's why I wanted to die with you on the toboggan.'

(discontent with life), a 1980s equivalent of the romantic *mal du siècle*.

The aborted romantic scenario of Suzanne's failed relationship with Luc pales in importance beside the impossible incestuous love that colours the relationship between father and daughter. 'Mon père, je l'adore' Suzanne tells one of her lovers. Certainly the overtones of seduction that Alain Philippon remarks on in the collaboration between director and his protégée reflect the complex relationship that developed between Pialat and Bonnaire – 'Qu'il y ait une espèce de recherche de possession très proche du désir amoureux, oui, mais ce sont des rapports esthétiques quand même',[10] Pialat maintained (Pialat 1984: 11).

Significantly, *A nos amours* was only one of a number of films in the 1980s that were based on a father–daughter storyline, often with incestuous overtones. Vincendeau suggests that this stemmed partly from conditions inside the film industry during this period: ageing New Wave directors focused on increasingly younger heroines, while the dominance of older established male stars helped to maintain the 'imbalanced gender power relationship at the roots of the father–daughter narrative'. The attention paid to the father–daughter narrative also reflected the fact that within French society 'genetic engineering and changes in inheritance laws [...] put the position of the father within the family in crisis' (Vincendeau 1992: 16)). As work by Vincendeau, Noël Burch and Geneviève Sellier demonstrates, the father–daughter scenario has a long tradition in French cinema history, constituting what might be called a master narrative of mainstream cinema, coloured by prevailing social and political conditions but ultimately representing an assertion of paternal authority and patriarchal values. Only those in marginal positions: women, immigrants, avant-garde filmmakers among them, challenge this mainstream master narrative (Vincendeau 1992: 17). Pialat, neither a mainstream nor a marginal player, constructed the father's role out of two contradictory autobiographical models: the absent but powerfully present father of Langmann's narrative, and the father who is present but guilty of a form of abandonment in *La Gueule ouverte*. Not surprisingly, the film both reaffirms and subverts the father–daughter master narrative.

---

10 'That there is a kind of attempt at possession very close to that of amorous desire, yes, but it is an aesthetic relationship all the same.'

A key figure in the affirmation of patriarchal values is Marcel Pagnol, whom the father cites as a model for his son's writing. The father is at the centre of the social and moral order in Pagnol's universe. In fact, Burch and Sellier describe Pagnol's very popular 1937 film, *La Femme du boulanger*, as 'une véritable apologie de l'ordre incestuo-patriarcal, dont "tout le monde sait qu'il est contre nature" mais dont le maintien serait la condition de la paix civile et de l'unité nationale'[11] (Burch and Sellier 1996: 43). Pialat unquestionably admired Pagnol, despite what he dismissed as his 'prêchi-prêcha paternaliste' ('paternalist sermonising') because Pagnol told simple yet powerful and moving stories that reached a wide public (Pialat 1983: 7). The very fact that Pialat decided that the father, after being absent for one-third of the film, should return to sit down at the family table suggests a Pagnolesque reaffirmation of the traditional order. However, instead of bringing peace and stability the father deliberately sows discord and is driven away by his wife. Yet this does not result in the wife/mother's taking either his power or his place.

Abandoned by her husband and involved almost exclusively in domestic quarrels that often escalate to scenes of hysterical violence (she is never filmed in an exterior shot) the wife/mother is sacrificed to the father–daughter narrative. In Langmann's scenario, Evelyne Ker's role would inevitably have had considerably greater importance. However, the mother's isolation in the home, her anger and frustration, her hysterical lashing out at Suzanne, also reflected the conditions on the set. Pialat's admiration for Sandrine Bonnaire no doubt intensified his disappointment in Ker's more histrionic performances. As in the case of Cyr Boitard's Luc, when her work fell short of his expectations he lost interest in her character.

As Pialat's cinematographer Jacques Loiseleux reported, one take of a scene forced Ker to languish in bed on the set for at least three hours; a cut she received during one of the more violent confrontations required stitches. Yet in at least one scene Loiseleux found her expression of anger so excessive as to be embarrassing, almost grotesque, and he himself made the decision to move the camera to another room and stop filming her (Loiseleux 1983: 13). The slap that Ker gives her fictional husband in the penultimate scene was

11 'a veritable apology for the incestuo-patriarchal order which "everyone knows is against nature" but which is necessary in order to maintain civil order and national unity'.

unplanned, and directed as much towards Pialat the director as towards his character. Pialat later admitted that he was equally furious with her when he subsequently pushed her down on the table and he had no idea how far things would go (Pialat 1983: 6). Some viewers found Ker's hysterical performances particularly distasteful. However, as Ginette Vincendeau argues, Ker's character expresses the 'frustration and anger of a woman protagonist who is repeatedly defined as useless, full of love that is no longer needed,' a situation that finds a symbolic equivalent in her cooking meals that no one will eat (Vincendeau 1990: 265).

The place of the son becomes equally problematic – despite the fact he succeeds his father as head of the household – because he is portrayed as inadequate, displaying both incestuous and homosexual tendencies. As Pascal Mérigeau suggests, the choice of Dominique Besnehard to play Claude Berri's role already indicated that Pialat's relationship with the Langmann family was no longer wholly cordial. Claude Berri not only rejected Pialat's portrayal of his family but resented being represented by someone who resembled him so little, physically or psychologically – Besnehard's homosexuality was not a secret – and who was not even a professional actor. (Mérigeau 2002: 202). For his part, Besnehard lamented that a whole dimension of his character completely disappeared during the editing: 'Ce qui est fou c'est qu'il [Pialat] règle ses comptes à travers le cinéma; il n'avait pas envie que le personnage se justifie'[12] (Pialat 1984: 157).

However, the encouragement that Pialat gives his son in the film reflects real admiration for Berri's gifts as a writer. Pialat compared Berri to Pagnol in his facility for writing dialogue, and the parallel was reinforced because Berri was then working on his adaptation of Pagnol's *Jean de Florette*. The connection between the father/director and the son becomes important precisely because art is crucial to their identity. Suzanne shows no artistic talent or inclinations, admiring the work of her favourite painter, Bonnard, for its sensuality. The fact that Bonnard is most well known for scenes of domestic tranquillity has its irony, but further suggests that her taste in art is an extension of her sexuality. By contrast, all of the men in the film (not counting Suzanne's more episodic lovers) earn their livelihood through some

12 'What is crazy is that he [Pialat] settles scores through his films; he didn't want the [Berri] character to justify himself.'

form of artistic practice, whether they are artisans, like Suzanne's father and her husband Jean-Pierre; writers, like Robert and Jacques, or involved in the theatre, like Michel. Even Luc is studying drawing. This suggests the inferiority of the female characters, and although Suzanne will escape at the end of the film – both from her marriage and the repressive influence of her family, symbolically subverting the master narrative – she seems to require her father's permission to have a life of her own. Ultimately she owes her freedom and independence to his generosity, although he is not quite generous enough to allow her to go without reproaching her for what she fears most, having 'a dry heart'. His reproach suggests an underlying ambivalence towards her, which he overcomes in order to urge her to live fully, and this ambivalence also extends to his son.

It is through the relationship between the father and the son that the penultimate scene suddenly veers from being a family quarrel into being Pialat's own artistic profession of faith, an expression of his disgust over the corrupting power of money and his anger over the influential role of critics in creating and destroying reputations. The exchange between Pialat and Fieschi's characters takes on considerable importance by deliberately calling attention to the fact that latent in the narrative is an *histoire à clef*.

Pialat's decision to reintroduce his character in the penultimate scene was not common knowledge. He alerted the cameramen, borrowed a raincoat and walked onto the set, putting his actors on the spot – their surprise and consternation were unrehearsed. Pialat's attack on 'the brother-in-law' is overdetermined in Freudian terms, condensing his anger and resentment towards Jean-Pierre Rassam as well as his anger over Fieschi's having published an article in *Cinématographe* by Pierre-William Glenn (Pialat's cinematographer on *Passe ton bac d'abord*) in which Glenn claimed Pialat only merited three points (out of a possible twenty) as an artist. Caught off-guard, Fieschi was forced to improvise a response, unable to get up and leave because soundwires ran up inside his jacket and attached him to the table (Fieschi 1983: 19).

Most viewers remain unaware of this subtext, even though the very personal quality of Pialat's attack creates intense malaise and gives the scene its edge. What emerges in the film is the father's anger and disgust that his son has put success ahead of his art, and associated with self-serving critics and financial interests only too eager to exploit his talent – a situation aggravated by the fact that some of them are part of the family. On one hand, the father's attack is breathtakingly inappropriate, surly and mean spirited, particularly given the fact that his own position in regard to the family is hardly above reproach. Yet what gives his position credibility, despite his willingness to take advantage of the guests, is the force of his belief in the value of his son's art – the ability to create characters that 'live, that exist' – and in the need to defend it against the power of the establishment and of money. It is this, and the force of Pialat's own presence, that lead Robert's wife to conclude bemusedly 'C'est impressionnant quand même,' ('it's impressive all the same') after the father's forced departure.

During this scene Pialat treats his son as a traitor, yet he defends him against 'the brother-in-law', expressing outrage over the son's situation, outrage that is all the more powerful because it is Pialat's own outrage. Pialat assumes contradictory positions during this scene, speaking both for the father and for the son, without identifying fully with either. Neither a celebrated and popular artist, associated with the 'fathers', like Pagnol; nor a rebellious son, like the highly successful directors of the New Wave, he attempts to take on both positions. However, the divisions between the father and the son in this scene allow Pialat to give coherent expression to the contradiction. As the father, he expresses admiration for the popular Saturday night cinema by praising Pagnol, while his son dismisses the past as 'chiant' ('boring') and claims that he loves things of the 'moment' – just as Pialat values the intensity of the present. Certainly Pialat's decision to play the role of the father (and the fact that he chose to grow a beard during this period of his life) emphasises his maturity. However, he is not willing to take a back seat to a younger generation because, as he tells Suzanne in the final sequence, he is not 'all washed up yet'. In his late maturity he admires all the more the beauty of vital living things, eagerly imagining schools of whales off the coast of San Diego.

Style and form

The final sequences of *A nos amours* are 'pure' Pialat in the sense that they were his additions to Arlette Langmann's scenario, scenes he envisioned, developed and interpreted. He plays a major role in them, effectively competing with Suzanne as the film's narrative centre. Yet as René Prédal suggests, 'cinématographiquement les deux passages semblent tournés par des cinéastes différents'[13] (Prédal 1999: 110). The first, largely improvised, if rhythmed by the repetition of certain key phrases, takes place in the central décor of the film: the sombre, closed space of the Paris apartment whose central living area and workshop constitute the formal equivalent of a stage, the employees occasionally providing an audience for the action. Robert underscores the theatrical quality of the space, claiming after the first of the three scenes of hysterical violence 'que c'est pire qu'au Théâtre de poche' (Philippon 1989: 32) ('it's worse than at the Théâtre de poche'). During the interior shots, the camera moves in among the characters, smoothly tacking and shifting to follow the protagonists as it captures the action, frequently in long takes. By contrast, the action in the final scenes of the film takes place in sunny, public places, the street and the aisle of a moving bus, and the stationary camera registers the characters' delivery of a carefully written text. If the contrast between his approach to these two sequences suggests both Pialat's desire to capture ephemeral realities and his ideal of formal perfection, it also underscores his pragmatism. However, both sequences provide crucial examples of the increasing importance of ellipsis in his work.

Although Pialat's character laments the passage of time: 'A là là, le temps passe' ('Ah la, la, time flies'), he says ruefully in an early sequence, there are relatively few clues as to the period of time covered by the film. If, during the reception, the viewer learns that some six months have elapsed since Suzanne's last meeting with Luc – the sequence that immediately precedes the reception – and the reception itself, nothing prepares the viewer for the fact that Robert has been married in the interval. Nor is it immediately possible to identify his wife and brother-in-law, although a preternaturally alert viewer might have noticed that their characters were present on the boat in the early scenes from the summer camp. Pialat frequently dismissed interviewers' questions about his use of ellipsis by blaming a lack of preparation or foresight that left him without material to create transitional scenes. Ironically then, his character warns Robert about the importance of continuity. 'Faut que ça raccorde' ('the cuts must match'), he admonishes Robert, as his son is about to begin

13 'cinematographically, the two passages appear to be filmed by different filmmakers'.

cutting some furs. However, by the time Pialat made *A nos amours* this 'weakness' had become one of the most striking formal elements of his work.

In fact, in some cases he deliberately intensifies the impact of discontinuity by matching cuts, creating a deceptive link between one scene and another. Perhaps the most striking of these *faux raccords* is sequence 12, after the father's departure, when Suzanne returns home very late to find her mother sewing in the workroom. In one of their few affectionate exchanges, Suzanne urges her mother not to work so late, then announces that she is going to her room. The following shot shows her entering it, but in broad daylight, and she is wearing different clothes. This cut also heralds a change in tone, as mother and daughter almost immediately engage in a dispute that quickly grows violent as Betty becomes hysterical, slaps Suzanne, then attacks Robert as he tries to separate them. A similar break follows the third and most violent of the family quarrels. A shot of Suzanne in the street, her face wet with tears, initially leads the viewer to assume her distress reflects what happened in the previous sequence. However, Suzanne is tenderly consoled by a new character identified as Jean-Pierre, who has clearly known her for some time.

Another crucial gap precedes Suzanne's announcement of her departure for San Diego, a decision that catches the viewer as much off-guard as it does her father, even though it mirrors his earlier flight from the family. The film is brought to a close by the alternation (typical of all of Pialat's films to this point) between movement and stasis, between those who stay and those who leave. The contrapuntal movement of the final shots echoes that of *La Gueule ouverte*: the image of the father as his bus enters a tunnel is followed by a cut to Suzanne and Michel on the plane. However, the contrast between darkness and daylight, the waiting plane and the moving bus reverses the dynamics of *La Gueule ouverte*. The film ends with a shot that looks towards the future, yet Klaus Nomi's music rises again during the credits, suffusing the new beginning with the poignancy of loss.

Police

The impetus for the film that became *Police* was provided by a dinner to which Toscan du Plantier invited Pialat and Gérard Depardieu, hoping to re-establish cordial relations between them. With the backing of Gaumont and the presence of a major star, Pialat could aim for the commercial success that had eluded him since *Nous ne vieillirons pas ensemble*. His search for an appropriate vehicle led him to the *polar*, or detective film, which counted for one-quarter of the film production in 1981 (Austin 1996: 99). Pialat was certainly not unaware that a year earlier Bob Swaim's stylish *polar*, *La Balance* (starring Nathalie Baye and Philippe Léotard – who had worked with him on *La Gueule ouverte*) had attracted considerable attention and won a César.

Pialat took an option on an American detective novel, borrowing its French title, *À nos amours*, before abandoning the idea of an adaptation, primarily because of difficulties in transplanting the action to a French context. However, the project moved forwards because of Catherine Breillat. Originally hired to work on the adaptation, she had contacted a lawyer friend who worked in a Tunisian drug milieu in Belleville and begun assembling documentary material for a film based on his cases. She spent her nights in studying the work of the 'brigades territoriales' – special undercover police who infiltrated the drug milieu. She subsequently insisted that she had not invented a single line of the police interrogations (Breillat 2003: 43). In fact, Toscan du Plantier later claimed that Pialat had unknowingly courted disaster, unaware that the subject was 'too hot' and that some of the 'actors' were actually principals in a case that had not even gone to court (Toscan du Plantier 2003: 59).

The stature of the stars involved in *Police*, the power and influence of Gaumont, all contributed to greater public awareness of the conflicts that surrounded the film and played themselves out on the set. Pialat's conflicts with Breillat over the scenario (which led to a lawsuit) were followed by his difficulties with then teen idol Sophie Marceau. Marceau never accepted Pialat's approach to filming – finally retreating into what Pialat called a 'tower' of polite formality. Pialat's frustration with her emerges in the film where Depardieu/Mangin borrows Pialat's words, calling Noria a 'tour fermée' ('impenetrable tower') and accusing her of being unresponsive to his feelings (Pialat 1985c: 10).

Tensions on the set were not distributed exclusively along gender lines. Fireworks between Pialat and Richard Anconina (who played Lambert, the lawyer) stopped the filming on two occasions – once for almost two days (Mérigeau 2002: 240–2). On the other hand,

Depardieu's only major disagreement with Pialat concerned his refusal to model his character on real detectives. His Mangin remains an anomaly in the film, a wholly fictional character. Other characters were played by non-professionals, some real police officers, others discovered on location: at the corner bistro, or in local stores, like the elderly lady who picks her assailant out of a line-up. Bernard Fuzellier, who played the small-time thief whose nose Mangin breaks during an interrogation, was discovered by Catherine Breillat in a café in Belleville. To Fuzellier's surprise, he found himself being interrogated in the film by a real officer who had had dealings with him before (Fuzellier 1985: 20).

Despite the documentary nature of his material, Pialat dismissed critics who bracketed *Police* with Raymond Depardon's 1983 documentary film *Faits divers*, which followed the activities of police in the fifth arrondissement. *Police*, he claimed, was 'entièrement recomposé' (Pialat 1985: 15) ('entirely reconstructed'). Other than the exterior shots, only the restaurant scenes were done on location. Most of the film's action takes place in an abandoned school in Belleville where Pialat had sets constructed to represent the offices and holding cells of the 'brigade territoriale'. It provided the space he wanted, although conditions for lighting and sound were far from ideal. The large, low-ceilinged rooms were difficult to light, forcing Pialat's director of photography, Luciano Tovoli, to put together mobile groups of neon lights that he could move with the actors. Pialat was forced to dub the sound, going against his own longstanding practice, although he adhered closely to the actors' original delivery, even in cases where they stuttered or muffed their lines. Nonetheless, *Police* accelerates a shift in his attitude toward filming – 'je vais de plus en plus vers ce que je refusais avant,' he admitted, 'et ce film constitue une sorte de tournant pour moi'[14] (Pialat 1985b: 16).

Narrative and characterisation

Working to dismantle a Tunisian drug network with connections in Marseille, Inspector Mangin interrogates Tarak 'Claude' Laouati, who

14 'I am moving more and more towards what I rejected at first, and this film marks a kind of turning point for me'.

reveals his dealings with three brothers, 'Jean', 'Maxime' and 'Simon' Slimane. Tarak knows only the whereabouts of the youngest, 'Simon', who is living in Belleville with a *gauloise* named Noria. Mangin arrests both Noria and Simon, while Lambert, the Slimane family's lawyer (and a friend of Mangin's) attempts to free them. Lambert frequently meets his clients at 'René' El Gassah's Belleville café, where Mangin, unaware of René's key role in the drug network, is also a frequent customer. After Simon Slimane's arrest and interrogation he is taken into custody by the police in Marseille and held there pending his trial. Lambert claims that he can do nothing for Simon until his trial, but manages to free Noria, even though Maxime indicates the family does not care what happens to her. Meanwhile Maxime attempts to murder Tarak, but is seriously wounded. Accompanying Lambert to see Maxime at the hospital, Noria steals his keys in order to make off with a suitcase of the family's money and heroin. The family suspects both Noria and Lambert, although Noria swears to Simon that she did not take the money, and later denies it to Mangin as well.

When the family abducts and tortures Noria's brother, she appeals to Mangin, having in the interim become his mistress. He rescues her brother and attempts to protect her by hiding her at his apartment. Only when Lambert, completely unnerved (and unaware of Noria's presence), knocks on his door in the middle of the night after having been threatened by René, does Mangin learn that Noria has slept with Lambert and lied to both of them about the money. In order to save Noria from the family's vengeance, Mangin retrieves the bag of money and drugs and delivers it to René and Jean. When he returns to Noria, waiting in her car, she tells him that she is incapable of making him happy and must leave him. She offers him a final kiss, which he rejects. He walks away, returning to his apartment where the film ends as he turns towards the camera, his face a study of mixed emotions.

William Karel, a screenwriter who briefly replaced Catherine Breillat, could not have endeared himself to Pialat by insisting that the film's story was not sufficiently interesting to fill more than five lines on page ten of some scandal sheet. Pialat argued that 'l'important c'est de connaître les personnages' (Pialat 1985: 15) ('the important thing is to understand the characters'). Yet Pialat's interest in his characters comes at the expense of the violence and spectacular action sequences that remain a primary dramatic resource of the *polar*, and a major factor in its audience appeal. Only one shot is fired in the film – at night in a dark alley outside an illegal gambling establishment – as Maxime attempts to murder his family's betrayer. In fact, at the end of the film Mangin reveals that – for all his police training – he has never fired a shot at anyone. Pialat claimed there was no point in competing with American films on their home ground with the result that the film becomes an auteurist effort to remake the genre on his own terms (Pialat 1985c: 5). *Police* internalises the violence of the *polar*, making it a family affair – one family, constituted by the police, pitted against that of the Tunisian drug dealers. The violence is also more personal, even intimate, frequently played out during police interrogations, or in exchanges between betrayer and betrayed, whether in business or in love.

Where *Police* has some affinity with a tradition, it is not with the traditional *polar*, but with the poetic realist films of the 1930s that are French precursors of *film noir*, notably Renoir's *La Chienne or La Bête humaine*. *Police* reworks some of the key *noir* elements of this earlier tradition:

> a profound disillusionment with the unfulfilled promise of increasing urbanization, rationalization, and the rise of the money economy; an anxiety of self-definition centering on the frustrations of middle-class male protagonists; and the rise of a particular type of demonized 'new woman', the *femme fatale*, herself dubiously encoiled within the urban money economy. (Morgan 1996: 32)

The most obvious of these reworkings is the recasting of Noria as the manipulative and unfeeling *femme fatale* who betrays her lover Simon and ruins Mangin by leading him to betray his colleagues and compromise, perhaps 'fatally', his identity as an officer of the law. Pialat's claim that the film was initially Noria's story reflects the orientation of Breillat's script (Pialat 1985c: 10). Yet if Sophie Marceau's unwillingness to work with Pialat led to her character being displaced by Mangin, enough remains in the film to suggest that Noria's behaviour is coloured by a sense of betrayal and lingering bitterness over the failure of her relationship with Simon because his primary loyalty is to his family. Although she wears the hand of Fatima around her neck, and uses the name Noria, given to her by Simon, she remains an outsider in his world. Once Simon is incarcerated, his family openly expresses its suspicion and hostility, accusing her of being interested only in money, yet unwilling to earn it (through prostitution). Her failed assimilation is suggested by the fact that she spontaneously orders a ham sandwich while in police custody. She pays the family back for their rejection by stealing their drugs and money. Yet Noria also provides a mirror image (if an 'orientalist' and stereotyped one) of the Maghrebian family within the larger French culture. Ironically, she not only identifies with them, but becomes their strongest advocate in the film. She tells Mangin that she respects them because they have their own reality and their own truth.

As the central figure of the narrative, Mangin represents both the dominant cultural order and masculine worldview. The conflict between the system of law he represents and the 'alternative reality' of the Maghrebians, for whom a 'man's' word suffices, is constantly under-lined by the ritual of interrogation, where statements must be signed to have any legal validity – although the Maghrebians unofficial use of French first names compromises the procedure. Yet, as a represen-tative and defender of the social order, Mangin remains a problematic figure. Tough, sometimes brutal, he does not hesitate to rough up Noria when she replies insolently to his questions. His friendship with Lambert compromises him, as Lambert laughingly admits he has no compunction about defending his clients despite being convinced of their guilt. In a key exchange, emblematic of tangled *noir* plots, Mangin warns Lambert against getting involved with the prostitute Lydie, but lets himself be persuaded to arrest Lydie's troublesome pimp Dédé. He and Lambert take pleasure in the fact that if Mangin frames Dédé, the benighted Dédé will inevitably ask Lambert to defend him. Lambert will then not only get paid for putting a rival in jail for the maximum sentence, but have his victim thank him for doing it. Although Mangin enjoys the irony, claiming it is precisely the kind of little deal a cop finds irresistible because it hurts no one, except the guilty, he does not realise that it implicates him in a larger network of lies and betrayals that he, like the hapless Dédé, does not suspect.

Marginalised socially by his profession, compromised yet not corrupt, Mangin appears to run true to *noir* type. If Lydie mistakes him for a bourgeois, he has little in common with other bourgeois figures in Pialat's work. Yet he is sensitive about his status within the *Brigades territoriales*, although resigned to remaining an inspector. He scornfully dismisses the idea of passing exams or doing the three years of *culture générale* required to move up to *commissaire* like Marie Védret, who has neither his experience nor his street-smart credentials. Yet his apartment, recently redone – all black-market work – as he tells Lydie several times, includes a piano and suggests a cultured man who manages to live well. Moreover Mangin has two daughters (who never appear in the film) and might be expected to have a middle-class family life when off work – if it were not for the fact that he is a widower. This loss, unexplained, but linked to an undercurrent of sadness and vulnerability in Mangin's character, contrasts oddly with his macho stance, grossly sexist language and clumsy attempts to proposition almost every woman he meets. Surprisingly, he looks for love from Noria, who has already rejected two families, her own and Simon's, and who is hardly likely to choose married life with him. 'Tu me vois la femme d'un poulet?' ('Can you see me as the wife of a cop?'), she asks as they lie in bed together. His choice of the wrong woman points up one of the most frequently recurring themes of *film noir*: the non-fulfilment of desire (Morgan 1996: 39).

In *Police*, as in the pre-*noir* films of the 1930s, frustrated desire is linked to a realist portrayal of the corrupting power of money in the larger society. It is exemplified by the political influence of Turlot, 'the sugar king,' and the sexual perversity of Séverine's wealthy godfather, Grandmorin, in Renoir's *La Bête humaine*; or by Legrand's gradual descent into fraud and theft to sustain his relationship with his mistress Lulu (who in turn uses his money to pay for her pimp Dédé's fancy clothes and gambling debts) in his *La Chienne*. As Phil Powrie points out in his analysis of *Police* as a 1980s narrative of 'male discomfiture', *Police* – unlike Chabrol's or Corneau's polars of the 1980s – gives 'the spectator a critical view of the state of French society' (Powrie 1997: 96).

This comes into focus in the final bedroom conversation between Noria and Mangin, where each derides the other's dream of happiness. While Mangin feels life on an inspector's salary is not so bad, Noria points out that he could never in his entire working lifetime make as much money as he is about to return to the Maghrebians. He retorts that her idea of the good life is to take the money, sit on a beach somewhere under a coconut tree with a lover and have someone bring her drinks. Although she counters that a few interrogations and stake-outs are hardly better, he insists that it is a real life. If his attitude is both racist and sexist, he rejects easy money and empty pleasures in favour of the value of work well done, his pride in his department's excellent police work emerging earlier in his conversations with Lambert. Yet he remains profoundly pessimistic, rephrasing Chardonne to assert that 'le fond de tout est horrible' ('At bottom everything is rotten'). The reference suggests wide-ranging reading habits and a philosophical bent somewhat out of character for Mangin, but the quotation is clearly a pendant to Pialat's citation of Van Gogh's 'la tristesse durera toujours' in *A nos amours*. As Pialat's alter ego, Mangin conveys his ambivalence about working within a system (whether the police or the French film industry) where the corrupting influence of money can negate the value of good work. 'Il est évident qu'il y a actuellement une place vacante dans le cinéma français, et vous pouvez le prendre', an interviewer at *Positif* told Pialat when *Police* came out.[15] However, *Police* clearly conveys his ambivalence about taking that 'empty place'; the film provides not only a critical reflection on French society in the mid-1980s but, as Jean-Michel Frodon points out, a portrayal of the filmmaker's situation in the context of cinema history at the time (Frodon 1995: 743).

If Mangin were not a stand-in for Pialat, it would be more surprising – particularly given both genre conventions and the tradition of poetic realism – that Pialat chose not to resolve the web of narrative conflicts in *Police* by murder or death. By contrast, in a sequence added at the last minute, he turns the potential for a violent ending into a generous gesture. After Mangin delivers the money and drugs to René and heads back to Noria's car, a man hails him as he passes a café. Mangin hesitates, but the man insists he come in and have a drink. The situation appears to be a set-up, particularly as the man identifies himself as the suspect whose nose Mangin broke earlier. However, he and Mangin drink to the birth of his son, and Mangin discovers the boy will be given his own middle name, Vincent. A brief digression, without repercussions, the scene reflected Bernard Fuzellier's very real pride in the expected birth of his second child – 'a male' – as he tells Mangin in the course of their brief exchange. However, the scene also evokes and dismisses the expectation of violence attached to the genre. The final close-up of Mangin's solitary anguish overshadows this brief moment of community, but does not negate it.

15 'It is evident that there is an empty place in French cinema and you can take it.'

Style and form

Police is devoid of any of the facilities – the running jokes about Belgians or flamboyant dramatic climaxes to individual sequences typical of *La Balance*, for example – with which more commercial films appeal to viewers. Even scenes that might have been played for their irony or oblique comedy: Noria's ordering a ham sandwich, or René's ranting to Lambert that France is a pathetic country because it has no mafia, are not exploited dramatically. Nothing is explained, and much remains disconcerting. Pialat avoided the opening and closing of doors he disliked in *Loulou* by cutting into exchanges already under way, undismayed by potential ambiguities.

The narrative is no less fragmented for being more developed and is effectively cut in two by a three-month hiatus while Noria is held by the police in Marseilles. The first section of the film focuses on police work, the second on the relationship between Noria and Mangin. What links them is the primary figure of the film: the interrogation. There are in fact five separate interrogations: the interrogation of Tarak, which opens the film, that of Simon Slimane, followed by Noria's, then the thief's (Fuzellier) and finally René's. As Serge Toubiana points out, the interrogations and the love scenes are filmed in similar ways and pass through similar stages: confrontation, mutual testing/manipulation before culminating in a confession, although the process may include humiliation or intimidation. In the seduction scenes, 'il s'agit pour le mâle d'exhiber son désir sexuel ou sa demande d'amour, de faire pression pour que la femme en retour avoue qu'au fond, elle ne verrait pas ça d'un mauvais œil'[16] (Toubiana 1985: 11). Pialat experimented with moving in closer to his characters during the interrogations, advancing into the scene rather than panning to follow the actors. However, in the two seduction scenes he adopts a configuration that harks back to *Nous ne vieillirons pas ensemble* – both of these scenes take place inside a car, the tight framing and frame within a frame once again suggesting entrapment or imprisonment. Noria will move from the police holding cell to Mangin's embrace, although the 'truth' of her final confession sets her free.

16 'it is a question of the man's exhibiting his sexual desire or demand for love, and exerting some pressure on the woman to admit that basically she wouldn't be unwilling to go along with it'.

'Ce qui étonne dans *Police*, wrote a reviewer, c'est l'économie: deux, trois décors, assez nus, des cadres resserrés autour du visage des acteurs, un Paris sans Paris'[17] (Goldschmidt and Dazat 1985: 12). Another claimed the film was 'une pure construction géométrique' ('a pure geometric construction'), its vaunted contemporary realism an illusion (Frodon 1995: 743). If the film seems both pared down, yet rich in social detail, this is due in part to Pialat's combining short focal lengths – bringing him in close to his characters – with considerable depth of field (Pialat 1985: 20). This is echoed in the narrative by the fact that small details – desultory conversations, a tattoo that says 'j'aime ma petite fille' ('I love my little girl') or a hand of Fatima – evoke the world of memories and past experiences that each character brings into the film. Mangin's brief exchange with another cop about the war in Indochina, apparently gratuitous, suggests the way each of the characters represents the intersection of a personal story with national history.

The final freeze frame provides an example of the unusual importance Pialat sometimes attributed to narrative fragments. The image (a close-up of Depardieu, his expression a complex study of competing emotions) was salvaged from an exchange between Mangin and his housekeeper eliminated during the editing – in fact, the housekeeper herself completely disappeared from the film (Dedet 1985: 23). Consequently the emotions Depardieu displays were in no way related to the filmic events that supposedly produced them – the break-up with his lover Noria and their final goodbye in the preceding sequence. Pialat's attachment to this image led him to push the film slightly beyond the conventional limits of the plot by following Mangin back to his apartment after his final separation from Noria. This briefly raises the possibility that the narrative might take an entirely different turn, although this is immediately foreclosed by the freeze frame. If the freeze frame invests Depardieu's emotional turmoil with greater intensity by denying it full expression, the extradiegetic music which accompanies the final images both echoes and projects his anguish. This final image consummates the film's break with a genre narrative that began by typing Mangin as tough and cynical, a 'macho' male.

Police exceeded Pialat's initial expectations, drawing over a million and a half viewers, and bringing Gérard Depardieu an award at the

17 'What is astonishing in *Police* is its economy: two or three décors, rather bare, the tight framing of the actors' faces, a Paris without Paris.'

Venice Film Festival. As Daniel Toscan du Plantier recalled, the film came out just as he was fired by Gaumont, inspiring Depardieu and Pialat to plan another film so that he could continue to work as a producer. They huddled together at Depardieu's home in Trouville and decided to try for the Palme d'or (Toscan du Plantier 2003: 59).

References

Austin, Guy (1996), *Contemporary French Cinema*, Manchester, Manchester University Press.

Bergala, Alain (1983), 'Maurice Pialat, un marginal du centre', *Cahiers du cinéma*, no. 354.

Breillat, Catherine (2003), 'Témoignages', *Cahiers du cinéma*, no. 576.

Bonitzer, Pascal (1983), 'C'est vous qui êtes tristes', *Cahiers du cinéma*, no. 354.

Burch, Noel and Geneviève Sellier (1996), *La Drôle de guerre des sexes du cinéma français 1930–1956*, Paris, Nathan.

Dédet, Yann (1985), 'La Mémoire des rushes: entretien avec Yann Dédet', *Cahiers du cinéma*, no. 375.

Depardieu, Gérard (1988), *Lettres volées*, Lausanne, Editions J-C Lattès.

Fieschi, Jacques (1983), 'La Vie est à nous' *Cinématographe*, no. 94.

Frodon, Jean-Michel (1995), *L'Age moderne du cinéma français*, Paris, Flammarion.

Fuzellier, Bernard (1985), 'Tatouages', *Cinématographe*, no. 113.

Goldschmidt, Didier and Olivier Dazat (1985), 'Maurice Pialat: Interrogatoire', *Cinématographe*, no. 113.

Gonzalez, Christian (1985), *Gérard Depardieu*, Paris, Edilig.

Loiseleux, Jacques (1983), 'Entretien', *Cinématographe*, no. 94.

Magny, Joël (1992), *Maurice Pialat*, Paris, Cahiers du cinéma.

Mérigeau, Pascal (2002), *Pialat*, Paris, Editions Grasset & Fasquelle.

Morgan, Janice (1996), 'Scarlet Streets: *Noir* Realism from Berlin to Paris to Hollywood', *Iris*, no. 21.

Philippon, Alain (1983), 'La Débutante', *Cahiers du cinéma*, no. 354.

Philippon, Alain (1989), *'A nos amours' de Maurice Pialat*, Paris, Editions Yellow Now.

Pialat, Maurice (1980), 'Entretien', *Cinématographe*, no. 57.

Pialat, Maurice (1980b) 'Le Chercheur de la réalité: *Loulou*: entretien', *Positif*, no. 235.

Pialat, Maurice (1983), 'Entretien', *Cinématographe*, no. 94.

Pialat, Maurice (1983b), 'Le Chaudron de la création: entretien', *Cahiers du cinéma*, no. 354.

Pialat, Maurice (1984), *A nos amours: scénario et dialogue du film*, Paris, L'Herminier.

Pialat, Maurice (1985), 'Les Rayures du zèbre: entretien', *Cahiers du cinéma*, no. 375.

Pialat, Maurice (1985b), 'Interrogatoire', *Cinématographe,* no. 113.

Pialat, Maurice (1985c), 'Maurice Pialat sur le fil du rasoir: entretien', *Positif,* no. 296.

Prédal, René (1999), *'A nos amours': étude critique,* Paris, Nathan: Synopsis.

Powrie, Phil (1997), *French Cinema in the 1980s: Nostalgia and the Crisis of Masculinity,* Oxford, Oxford University Press.

Toscan du Plantier, Daniel (2003), 'Témoignages', *Cahiers du cinéma,* no. 576.

Toubiana, Serge (1985), 'L'Epreuve de la vérité', *Cahiers du cinéma,* no. 375.

Vincendeau, Ginette (1990), 'Therapeutic Realism: Maurice Pialat's *A nos amours'* in Vincendeau and Hayward (eds), *French Film: Texts and Contexts,* London/New York, Routledge.

Vincendeau, Ginette (1992), 'Family Plots: Fathers and Daughters', *Sight and Sound,* vol. 1, no. 11.

6

The saint and the artist: men apart

Like *Police, Sous le soleil de Satan* and *Van Gogh* reflect Pialat's move towards more ambitious projects in traditional genres. For all their differences in climate – *Sous le soleil de Satan* is a winter and nocturnal film; *Van Gogh*, despite its sombre ending, is lit by spring and summer sunlight – both films reflect a dominant trend in the 1980s, the heritage film, and pay homage to the tradition of studio film-making Pialat associated with the great filmmakers of his youth, Carné in particular. However, unlike Bertrand Tavernier's 1984 *Un dimanche à la campagne*, which marked a nostalgic return to the values of the tradition of quality (Powrie 1997: 13, 47–8), Pialat's films subvert the traditional forms in which they are cast.

Sous le soleil de Satan

Nothing could have seemed more astonishing than Pialat's decision to follow *Police* with an adaptation of Georges Bernanos's 1926 novel *Sous le soleil de Satan*. A novel of the 'supernatural incarnate' – complete with a false miracle – written by a fervent Catholic, it had impressed contemporary critics with its evocation of the mysterious reality of evil and of Satan (Estève 1987: 129, 131). Pialat, whose realism seemingly excluded supernatural or fantastic subjects, appeared to have mistaken himself for Robert Bresson. Yet the project had figured in Pialat's plans for over ten years. He originally envisaged doing an adaptation of what he considered 'le plus beau roman que j'ai jamais lu' ('the most beautiful novel I have ever read') in the early 1970s after

finishing *Nous ne vieillirons pas ensemble* (Chevassu 1990: 61). However, despite Pialat's conviction that the part of the priest, Donissan,
had practically been written for Depardieu, and that Bonnaire would
make an interesting Mouchette, rereading *Sous le soleil de* Satan with
an eye to adapting it made him all too aware of the potential
difficulties. He found the novel's supernatural elements less than
compelling and realised that crucial scenes lacked dialogue, while in
other scenes Bernanos's lyrical prose would demand a good deal of
his actors (Pialat 1987: 8).

Pialat's choice of Depardieu – as he appears in the role: heavy,
plodding, out of breath, seemingly dazed and frequently unsteady on
his feet – is emblematic of the difficulties faced by a realist filmmaker
attempting to portray the invisible and ineffable mysteries of faith and
of spiritual vocation solely through material means. If Pialat attempts,
once, to use voice-over to convey the priest's innermost thoughts, he
then abandons it as an option. There is no other articulation of the
priest's convictions, motivations, physical or spiritual anguish except
through his gestures, exchanges with others and the brief moments
in which he talks to himself. It is not surprising that Pialat saw his
adaptation as a struggle with the Bernanos novel from which he (and
Sophie Danton, credited with the scenario) ultimately wrested the
material necessary to create his film. 'Bresson s'est moins colleté, il
me semble' ('Bresson came less to grips with it, it seems to me'), he
told *Cahiers*, commenting on Bresson's fidelity to Bernanos in
adapting *Le Journal d'un curé de campagne* (Pialat 1987: 62). However,
Pialat's total engagement with the work led to his acting in the film,
where he took the role of the Doyen of Campagne, Minou-Segrais,
Donissan's superior and spiritual adviser.

Pialat's adaptation retained Bernanos's language (modified to
avoid archaic expressions) and the general framework of his novel.
However, working with a finished, predetermined narrative ran
counter to Pialat's normal approach, and he considered eliminating
the famous encounter with the devil before Bernanos's heirs objected
(Mérigeau 2002: 255). He did dispense with the supernatural shape-
shiftings that gave Donissan's struggle with Satan a metaphysical
reality in the novel. In fact, given the uncompromising realism of
Pialat's presentation of the events, nothing prevents the viewer
unacquainted with the novel from considering the experience a delu-
sion brought on by the priest's exhaustion and spiritual torment,

while the scene takes on overtones of sexual seduction that are at odds with Bernanos's text.

Two changes suggest Pialat's difficulties in coming to terms with the material and the failure of his original impulse to make this a film through which he could come to terms with the past, his own past and that of cinematic tradition. Pialat had asked Claude Berri to play the role of Dr Gallet, one of Mouchette's lovers, a choice intended to convey his respect for Berri and his work despite the anger and resentment expressed towards him in *A nos amours*. The choice seems particularly apt in retrospect as Berri went on to become the major director of heritage films in France in the late 1980s and 1990s. However, Berri's interaction with Sandrine Bonnaire was problematic and after a brief hiatus during which Pialat's cameraman fell ill and the shooting was halted, Pialat replaced Berri with his film editor, Yann Dedet (Mérigeau 2002: 257–8). More significant in terms of Pialat's faithfulness to Bernanos's text was the disappearance of Alain Cuny, an actor whose long career went back to Carné – he had played opposite Arletty in *Les Visiteurs du soir* during the Occupation. Cuny was engaged to play the role of the writer Saint-Marin, Bernanos's caricature of Anatole France, a writer whose Voltairian irony placed him at the opposite end of the spectrum from Bernanos's own metaphysical conception of art. In the concluding section of the novel, Saint-Marin hopes to arrange an audience with Donissan, expecting to debunk the saint for his readers. However, Bernanos condemns Saint-Marin's scepticism and his literary dilettantism by depriving him of the chance to attack the saint. The novel concludes as Saint-Marin discovers Donissan's body in the confessional. Pialat filmed scenes from the novel including Cuny as Saint-Marin, but later cut them. Instead, his own character, Menou-Segrais, discovers the priest's body.

Narrative and characterisation

Pialat's film folds the prologue of Bernanos's novel – the story of the pregnant sixteen-year-old Germaine Malorthy, called Mouchette, who impulsively shoots her lover, the Marquis de Cadignan, when he refuses to go away with her – into the central section of the novel, which introduces the priest Donissan. A priest of peasant stock, just out of seminary, Donissan's extreme awkwardness and excessive zeal confounds his superiors and disconcerts the parishioners of Campagne where he has been placed under the guidance of the Dean, Menou-Segrais. As the Dean learns when Donissan faints during a confrontation between them, the priest attempts to compensate for doubts about his vocation by excessive mortifications of the flesh that seriously weaken him. This section of Bernanos's novel also relates the two defining moments of Donissan's life, which are also key moments in the film: his meeting with the devil and his encounter with Mouchette.

Donissan encounters the devil when he loses his way after cutting across the fields to reach the neighbouring parish of Etaples. Increasingly exhausted and disoriented, he wanders in the cold and growing darkness until he is accosted by a friendly horse trader who offers to show him a shortcut. Too weak to go on, Donissan accepts the man's invitation to spend a night in a small hut where they can build a fire. Donissan falls asleep but wakes to find the horse trader bending over him, then recognises Satan in human form. After Satan kisses him, Donissan struggles with him and rejects his offer of greater self-knowledge. However, the trader claims that the priest has been given a special grace to see into the souls of others. Donissan wakes the next morning in the road, roused by a quarryman who claims that he and the trader had carried him there.

Walking back into Campagne in the early morning Donissan meets Mouchette, and tells her that he understands the nature of her crime and her despair. He says that she is innocent of Cadignan's murder, insisting she was merely a pawn in the hands of Satan, and exhorts her to turn to God. However, their meeting bewilders her and, growing increasingly anguished, she later kills herself, slitting her throat with her father's razor. Donissan, apparently having sensed her intention, breaks into her room, but is too late. He picks up her body and places it on the church altar in order to return her to God. The local bishop puts an end to the scandal by sending Donissan to the Trappist monastery for a period of several years. Donissan is subsequently named curé of the small provincial town of Lumbres, where his parishioners come to consider him a saint. Faithful to Bernanos, Pialat entirely elides the five years spent in the monastery, as well as the forty years of Donissan's work in Lumbres to focus on his last days as they are related in the final section of Bernanos's novel.

Called to the deathbed of a young boy by a mother who believes the saint can save him, Donissan once again arrives too late. However, he is tormented by the thought that he could or should try to resuscitate the child. Uncertain whether this impulse comes from God or from Satan, he remains paralysed by doubt until urged by another priest to save the boy. Slowly lifting the boy's body towards the crucifix above him, Donissan prays for God to triumph over Satan and raise the dead child, offering his salvation in exchange for the boy's life. The boy's eyes open, but when his mother sees this and cries out, Donissan puts the boy's still inert form back on the bed. As the film shows the boy's eyes open, some ambiguity remains (in the film, although not in the novel) as to whether a miracle has in fact occurred. Consequently it is not entirely clear from Pialat's adaptation that Donissan returns to Lumbres carrying the crushing weight of his failure. Alone in his room he will be, literally, felled by a heart attack. Sensing he is near death, Donissan prays to be allowed to stay in the world if he can still be useful to God, and the next shot shows him, unsteady on his feet, entering the church sanctuary.

During Donissan's absence, Menou-Segrais has come to visit his old friend – an event invented for the film. However, Menou-Segrais does not go immediately to greet Donissan, holding back discreetly when he sees Donissan open the church to waiting parishioners. Later the dean will go into the church to look for him, opening the door to the confessional to find the priest dead of a second heart attack. Light coming from above Donissan illuminates his face. After closing Donissan's eyes, then briefly caressing his cheek, Menou-Segrais walks back into the depths of the church, then turns and looks towards his friend. The final image is his vision of the saint, light streaming down over his face in the darkness of the confessional.

As in making *La Gueule ouverte*, if for very different reasons, there was both artistic and financial risk involved in Pialat's decision to adapt Bernanos's novel. Joël Magny considered it an impossible project (Magny 1992: 106). Yet the film defends the willingness to take important risks: 'La sagesse est le vice des vieillards' ('Wisdom is the vice of the old'), Menou-Segrais retorts when his bishop reproaches him for his part in the scandal created by Mouchette's suicide. In fact, the impulsive willingness to take such risks links both the director and his character to Donissan and Mouchette. The importance of the bond between Menou-Segrais and Donissan is emphasised by the priest's first words in the film: 'Quand je suis avec vous tout me paraît simple. Quand je suis tout seul je ne vaux rien'.[1] It is Menou-Segrais who will guide Donisson and use the word 'sainthood' in urging him to take a path that will force him to 'monter, monter, ou vous perdre' (Bernanos [1926] 1961: 134) ('climb, climb or be lost').

Pialat's Menou-Segrais is a complex character: perceptive, kind and generous, yet with a repressed anger that emerges in his hostility towards ecclesiastical authorities. Worldly (he does not forget to thank generous parishioners for their gifts, or neglect his creature comforts), he has considerable strength of character, and deliberately risks offending the church hierarchy, for which he has little respect, to promote his younger colleague's vocation. Bernanos's Menou-Segrais attempts to work his own spiritual salvation through Donissan, and the fact that it is Menou-Segrais who sends Donissan to Etaples, where he will meet the devil, gives the relationship a darker side. Pialat's Menou-Segrais will at one point literally have Donissan's blood on his hands – wiping it off with an irreproachably white handkerchief. However, where Bernanos's novel avoids any ambiguity in their relationship by having Menou-Segrais speak to Donissan on Christmas Eve – emphasising the Christ-like nature of the priest's vocation and the rightness of Menou-Segrais' counsel – Pialat does not dispel the ambiguity.

Pialat's Menou-Segrais pushes the priest into a role he did not dare envision, and abandons him to his fate: 'Je vous donne à ceux qui vous attendent et dont vous serez la proie'.[2] Alain Philippon observes that 'Lorsqu'à la fin du film Menou-Segrais découvre le cadavre de Donissan dans le confessionnal et lui ferme les yeux, tout se passe – aucun affect sur son visage – comme s'il contemplait son œuvre diabolique, l'achèvement de sa tâche mortifère'[3] (Philippon 1987: 5). As Philippon points out, Menou-Segrais is Donissan's 'metteur en scène', however, the film goes beyond the portrayal of self-sacrifice as the fulfilment of an individual vocation. Pialat's film suggests a post-

1 'When I am with you everything seems simple. When I am alone I am worthless.'
2 'I am giving you to those who are expecting you and whose prey you will be.'
3 'When at the end of the film Menou-Segrais finds Donissan's body in the confessional and closes his eyes, it appears – no expression on his face – as though he were contemplating his diabolical achievement, the completion of his deadly task.'

modern dimension to sainthood by conveying its public aspect, a form of celebrity suggested by the crowd of Donissan's parishioners at Lumbres jockeying for a position near the great man's carriage, hoping he will sign their religious images. The saint, the actor and the film director all share the burden of having a 'reputation', the danger of being trapped by it, and the risk of failing to measure up to their own and their public's expectations. If there is something vampiric in Menou-Segrais' role, the film intimates that his guilt is also shared by the public, believers and 'fans', sceptics or the merely curious, who would exploit the saint and tempt him to work miracles.

Mouchette is also crucial to Donissan's effort to become a saint, although Pialat articulates her continuing importance to the curé de Lumbres exclusively through the appearance of her ghost (the film's only touch of the supernatural other than the putative miracle) in the final section of the film. Bernanos's Mouchette gives herself up to the devil in her despair, although Sandrine Bonnaire's character remains more ambiguous because the viewer never learns what goes through her mind during the troubled moments immediately preceding her suicide. Her strength, her rebellion, her search for love and her suicidal urges make her a sister to Suzanne in *A nos amours*. Both move from lover to lover, although Mouchette's restlessness has a metaphysical dimension that she herself does not entirely understand: 'D'abord je ne me connaissais pas moi-même', she tells Cadignan, 'On est content sans savoir, d'un rien, d'un beau soleil, des bêtises, quoi. Mais enfin tellement content ... qu'on désire autre chose en secret. Mais quoi? C'est comme une chose ... sans elle le reste n'est rien'.[4] Her impulsive murder of Cadignan, perhaps motivated by his forcing himself on her sexually (although this too remains ambiguous in the film), has no repercussions as Cadignan's death is universally believed to be a suicide. When Mouchette meets Donissan, she is already slightly delusional, tormented by her crime and her inability to confess. Donissan's long harangue not only fails to convince her to return to God but precipitates her suicide. His sainthood becomes both an effort to expiate this failure and to ransom her soul.

The importance of the intersection of these two very different stories does not fully emerge in the film, but this is the result of

4 'At first I didn't understand myself. One is happy without knowing why, for no reason, a sunny day, stupid things. But finally so happy ... that we secretly desire something else. But what? It's like a thing ... without it the rest is nothing.'

Pialat's fidelity to the tripartite structure of Bernanos's novel. The novel begins with the story of Mouchette, complete in itself, which makes no mention of Donissan; the two characters meet only in the second section, while the final section focuses exclusively on Donissan and his work as the curé of Lumbres. The juxtaposition of the stories, which at first appear to have nothing to do with one another, may well have appealed to Pialat's own taste for ellipsis, although it is inevitably detrimental to conveying the interdependence of the two storylines in the film. However, Pialat finds a perfect formal equivalent for the paratactic quality of Bernanos's text: a brilliant and disorienting cut between Donissan's holding out a communion wafer as he gazes towards the back of the church, and, what initially appears to be a countershot, Mouchette's entry into what the viewer at first assumes to be the cathedral. It is instead Mouchette entering Cadignan's apartments.

Style and form

The film, like the novel, is structured by five nocturnal encounters, each marked by a confrontation or struggle: Mouchette's confrontation with Cadignan, Donissan's interview with Menou-Segrais, Donissan's encounter with the devil, followed by his encounter with Mouchette and finally his death in the darkness of the confessional. The timeframe for these events remains unclear, particularly as the characters' clothing does not suggest a particular time period, and neither Donissan nor Menou-Segrais appears to age. Menou-Segrais, supposedly at the end of his career when he counsels Donissan at the beginning of the film, could not realistically be expected to close the priest's eyes in death some forty years later. Yet, the drama gains in intensity for being condensed into a kind of eternal present, the priest's physical weakness in the early scenes merely merging into symptoms of his failing heart.

The carriages and farm wagons that move along the muddy roads leading towards Etaples give way towards the end of the film to a rattletrap truck that brings Donissan back to Lumbres from the visit to the dying child, but little else, other than the passage of night to day suggests the passing of time. The interplay of light and darkness is a formal constant of the film – repeating the contrast between divine illumination and the dark sun of Satan. This opposition plays an important formal role both in the drama of the failed resurrection, where the saint's gesture lifts the child up into the shadowy darkness of the room rather than into divine light; and in the apparent apotheosis of the saint at the end of the film. The shift between day and night also sets the stage for the crucial event of both the novel and the film, the encounter with Satan.

Donissan's departure for Etaples begins in daylight. It is the occasion for stunning shots of the countryside, unusual in Pialat's films, which presage the even greater beauty of his portrayal of nature in *Van Gogh*. An extreme long shot of Donissan in his black cassock walking along a muddy road under the arch of a bridge, followed by a heavy farm wagon drawn by massive percherons, has the character of an old master, all the more striking given Pialat's usual avoidance of the overtly aesthetic. The sequence also violates the 'human' scale of Pialat's previous work: the preponderance of long, medium-long and medium shots intended to reflect normal vision. If he also avoided jarring juxtapositions of long shots with close-ups – the latter relatively infrequent in his work – he again breaks with his usual practice, shifting from wide-angled panoramic shots of the priest – a tiny black figure lost (literally and figuratively) in the dizzying sweep of undulating fields – to medium, medium close-up and long shots of the plodding Donissan, filmed from both high and low angles, conveying both the daunting amount of territory to be covered and the priest's increasing exhaustion and disorientation. The sequence of these shots stretches out painfully, then a sudden cut brings darkness, and the horse trader's shadowy figure, visible behind the priest on the now level road, has materialised out of nowhere.

Pialat underlines the importance of their encounter – and the subsequent meeting with Mouchette – by having them take place in the countryside. The majority of the action is filmed in interior spaces. Here the play of light and darkness draws attention to the windows, which figure so prominently in interior shots that they become a motif (Durier 1991: 84). As the window offers an opening onto the life of the outside world and brings light into darker or closed interior spaces, it is significant that the windows in the film are either closed, or, in the confrontation between Cadignan and Mouchette, about to be closed. However, the window, as a connection to the outside world, is ultimately replaced by the door to the dark coffin-like space of the confessional which Donissan closes on himself in the final scene. Only the white rays which bathe the saint's face after his death suggest an escape into eternal light.

There are moments in the film which recall the more improvisational, documentary approach of Pialat's earlier films – a brief moment when Menou-Segrais teases a group of young women about gossiping during mass, for example. However, Pialat's desire to measure himself against both an older studio tradition and more polished 'commercial' films leads him to be particularly attentive to the formal qualities of the film. This desire to show his mastery of the medium also explains Pialat's willingness to resort to special filters or special effects (day for night in the encounter with Satan) and to consider post-synchronisation in order to obtain greater sound clarity. Despite his earlier aversion to introducing extradiegetic music – although it figures briefly in *A nos amours*, and during the final scene of *Police* – he uses the 'Intermezzo' of Henri Dutilleux's *First Symphony* to a much greater extent in *Sous le soleil de Satan*. It not only serves to evoke an emotion, but to carry a scene. He also makes striking, even daring, use of sound: the violent crash of Donissan's breaking down the door to Mouchette's bedroom substitutes for the visual violence of her suicidal gesture.

By contrast, the final image of the film seems predictable, a melodramatic triumph of light over darkness, a visual confirmation of the saint's attainment of glory. Yet the full weight of the film works against the final image, the saint's life marked by a series of failures concluding with the denial of his final prayer. Menou-Segrais had earlier offered Donissan a cautionary assessment of the uselessness of the saint in times when 'les hommes ne recherchent que l'agréable et l'utile – dans un tel monde il n'y a plus pour le saint, ou alors on dit qu'il est fou'.[5] The inclusion of the writer Saint-Marin might have underlined this still further. The film's final image seems to represent a regressive, but failed attempt to preserve the value of sainthood in a world where even Menou-Segrais/Pialat sees no real place for the saint. This regression is precisely what constituted the beauty of the film for Serge Toubiana: 'La beauté bizarre du film de Pialat – elle a dérangé Cannes, c'est le moins qu'on puisse dire – vient de ce détour,

---

5 'people are only looking for the agreeable and the useful – in such a world there is nothing for the saint, or else they say he is a madman'.

ou du retour à une France insondable, archaïque, à la fois populaire et noble, simple et grandiloquante'[6] (Toubiana 1987: 7).

Pialat's film won the Palme d'or for France for the first time in over twenty years, but the decision was controversial. Pascal Mérigeau suggested that Alain Cavalier's surprisingly popular 1986 film *Thérèse*, about Thérèse de Lisieux, which presented a more smiling vision of sainthood, may have created a climate in which Pialat's tormented characters were less well received (Mérigeau 2002: 255). However, opposition to the film came from those who might have been expected to appreciate it most: Bernanos specialists and conservative Catholics who argued that the film betrayed the novel or at the very least fell short of conveying the supernatural quality of the saint's vocation as a follower of Christ (Estève 1995: 91, 98). Their disapprobation was echoed by critics like Gérard Lenne, who took no interest whatsoever in Bernanos's vision of sainthood, claiming in *La Revue du cinéma* that 'Nous n'entrons jamais ... dans le drame intérieur de l'abbé Donissan [...] prêtre obsédé, dévoué à Satan, qui converse avec le Malin et voit apparaître des fantômes'[7] (Lenne 1987: 38). This double opposition suggests the problematic positioning of the film. *Sous le soleil de Satan* successfully upheld the cultural prestige of the literary adaptation, but failed to win over the general public. Serge Toubiana's defence of the award in *Cahiers du cinéma* merely underlined the cultural resistance to the film: 'L'argument le plus stupide, le plus haïssable, développé de long en large par la droite (*Figaro, Quotidien de Paris*) pour attaquer à la fois le jury et le film de Pialat, a consisté à dire qu'il était dangereux d'attribuer un Palme d'or à un film qui n'allait pas à priori avec le goût immédiat du public'[8] (Toubiana 1987: 7).

Not quite ten years later in his last interview with *Cahiers du cinéma*, Pialat dismissed the film as 'academic' (Pialat 2000: 59). It is arguably neither his least personal work (the title might go to *Police*),

6 'The bizarre beauty of Pialat's film – it disturbed Cannes, to say the least – comes from this detour or return to an unfathomable, archaic France, both popular and noble, simple and grandiloquent'.

7 'We never get involved ... in the internal conflict of abbé Donissan [...] obsessed priest, devotee of Satan, who converses with the Evil one and sees ghosts.'

8 'The most stupid and hateful argument, expounded widely by conservatives (in the newspapers the *Figaro* and the *Paris Daily*) to attack both the jury and Pialat's film, consisted in saying that it was dangerous to attribute the Palme d'or to a film that a priori was not in step with the current taste of the public.'

nor (despite the Palme d'or) his most successful, yet it reflects an extraordinary energy and ambition in the desire to create the artisan's equivalent of a masterwork, visible proof of his own calling. If Pialat went so far as to regret his award, feeling it was somehow compromised, he could not deny the importance of the recognition. Moreover, the Palme d'or allowed him to pull together the resources to make another film that had long interested him, a film on Van Gogh.

Van Gogh

Pialat frequently asserted that Nicolas Poussin was his favourite painter, but admitted that he had adored Van Gogh when he was in his twenties (Pialat 1992: 107). The idea for a film on Van Gogh first emerged during the 1960s when Pialat made a short film for French television on the town of Auvers-sur-Oise, seeing it through the eyes of famous painters who had worked there. Yet there are certainly suggestions that the painter continued to be important to Pialat. Not only is Van Gogh quoted in *A nos amours*, it is not impossible to see other references to the painter in the fact that Vincent was the name given the baby adopted in *L'Enfance nue*, or that there is a toast to another child named Vincent at the end of *Police* when Mangin reveals that Vincent is also his middle name. However, Pialat might never have made a film about Van Gogh if Daniel Auteuil had not expressed the desire to make a film with the director of *Sous le soleil de Satan*. Auteuil was enthusiastic about playing Van Gogh, but the project simmered for a year as it was too late to begin filming that summer. Then Auteuil's commitment to the Avignon Theatre Festival led to conflict with Pialat and to Auteuil's eventually abandoning the project.

Pialat's decision to move forward, replacing Auteuil with Jacques Dutronc meant the film would take an entirely different direction. Dutronc, who had become famous as a rock musician and composer in the 1960s, projected a persona very different from the tortured, emotive character ascribed to the legendary artist. Cool, aloof, sardonic, often photographed with a large cigar clenched in his teeth at a rakish angle, Dutronc was viewed as the exact opposite of a Depardieu or an Auteuil. While not an amateur, having made some fourteen films before working with Pialat, Dutronc did not dominate the screen. Reserved and diffident, he seemed to make films as though he were travelling in foreign territory where he was uncertain of his welcome (Joyard and Larcher 2000: 57). As Joël Magny points out, the question of whether to believe in Dutronc as a credible Van Gogh becomes an extension of the question that inevitably was at issue for Théo, Dr Gachet or anyone in Auvers who knew the painter – was Van Gogh merely a troubled man, or was he a genius? (Magny 1992: 34).

As with many of his other films, Pialat chose more seasoned actors for the primary roles, but expanded the universe of the film with amateurs. Didier Barbier, who played the village idiot, was Jacques Dutronc's secretary, while Lise Lamétrie, who played the wife of the owner of the *pension Ravoux*, was actually the *gardienne* of the Pialats' Paris apartment building (Mérigeau 2002: 295–7). Pialat was no doubt pleased that the ample budget allowed for costumes and period sets for almost an entire village. However, he would later estimate that as much as one-third of the money was wasted because the sets were either not ready when he needed them, or they were 'abominable' and he refused to use them (Pialat 1992: 105). Consequently, the film does not anchor the events in the town of Auvers or attempt to emphasise period detail, relying instead on a vague 'pastness' that does not distance the emotional force of the events.

Narrative and characterisation

Pialat's film opens as Van Gogh steps off a train in Auvers-sur-Oise in mid-May of 1890, just two months before his suicide. These last months represented an incredibly productive period for the artist who appeared to be recovering his mental and physical equilibrium. Absorbed in painting Auvers and its surroundings, he completed some seventy-six paintings. However, unlike other serious screen biographies of Van Gogh (Minelli, 1956; Cox, 1987; Altman, 1990), Van Gogh's art, and the nature of his artistic creation have relatively little importance in Pialat's film. Instead, Pialat drew on documentary materials to reconstruct the painter's relationships with the small society of family, friends and neighbours that would ultimately fail to save him, most notably his brother Théo and his wife Jo, and Dr Gachet, the doctor in whose care Vincent places himself in the final weeks of his life. While Dr Gachet is remembered primarily because of Van Gogh's famous portrait of him, Van Gogh also painted his daughter, Marguerite Gachet, and she has the final word on the painter in Pialat's film. It is not an expression of her admiration for his artistic genius, but her assertion that he was her friend.

The narrative follows the painter's story closely in some respects, showing his day-to-day life in Auvers, and his relationship with the Ravoux family from whom he rented a room. It recreates a documented visit by Théo and Jo to the Gachets, as well as the tensions between Vincent and Théo over money and Théo's inability to sell his brother's paintings. Yet Pialat also reworks Van Gogh's story by suggesting that he was neither anguished and mentally unstable nor physically ill. The famous incident of the severed ear, which would have emphasised Van Gogh's torment and self-destructive urges, is barely alluded to in the film. Pialat's Dr Gachet claims to find Vincent in reasonable physical health, merely exhausted by the intensity of painting constantly, the abuse of absinth and a poor diet. He tells Théo that Vincent's 'attacks' might be closer to hysteria – which, he assures Théo, is not exclusively a feminine malady. To his daughter, Gachet represents the situation somewhat differently, recalling the months in an asylum in Saint Rémy and the painter's slashing off his ear, but refusing to pronounce Vincent either sane or insane. Vincent himself insists to Théo (against all biographical evidence) that his attacks were merely defensive manoeuvres equivalent to a squid's ejection of ink.

Pialat's quasi dismissal of the importance of Van Gogh's psychological instability parallels the complete elimination of the spiritual or metaphysical anguish which is as much a part of the artist's legend as the final dark painting of a wheatfield with crows. Henri Perruchot, whose popular biography, *La Vie de Van Gogh*, Pialat might even have consulted, ascribes the artist's suicide to profound despair that had both metaphysical and material causes. Perruchot quotes one of Van Gogh's letters to his brother just over a year before his suicide, in which Vincent assured Théo he would repay him for his support: 'Je rendrai l'argent ou je rendrai l'âme' ('I'll give back the money or give up my life'). 'Il n'a pas rendu l'argent,' Perruchot writes, continuing:

> Inutile a été la moisson forcénée des chefs-d'œuvre ... inutile la quête des grands secrets. Inutile la ferveur. Car tout est inutile. La Connaissance est un serpent qui se dévore. Au-delà du Champ de blé aux corbeaux, que pouvait-il y avoir? Il n'y a rien que cet épouvantable

néant auquel répond l'amer silence d'un homme.[9] (Perruchot 1955: 466–7)

Perruchot's description perpetuates the romantic view of the artist as a prophet, a 'voyant' or a seer, a mythic view that places value on the artwork both as a form of revelation and the product of a difficult, painful and possibly destructive effort to reach an ultimate truth. However, this mythic, metaphysical view of art is at odds with the postmodern conception of a fully commodified artwork, an object of exchange whose value fluctuates with market demand. By emphasising Van Gogh's inability to sell his work, Pialat translates the painter's tragedy into postmodern terms.

The importance of money and markets in the tragedy is also confirmed by hard fact: the painter's inability to sell more than a single painting during his lifetime. However, Pialat's film also condemns Théo for being at least partly responsible for Vincent's failure. For although he sacrifices to support his brother financially, Pialat's Théo does not see the value of Vincent's work, admitting privately to his wife that he wished Vincent painted more like Renoir. Perhaps unconvincing when he tries to sell art that he himself does not appreciate, Théo is unable to market his brother's paintings. Pialat then represents Van Gogh's death as a 'family' tragedy, the consequence of the painter's betrayal by bourgeois critics and art dealers, first among them his brother.

Consequently, although Vincent continues to paint, expending his energy and talent, he receives nothing in return, a dimension of his situation that Pialat conveys, without any suggestion of the metaphorical, through a kind of physical 'diminishment' associated with 'hunger' – both made visible by Dutronc's emaciated appearance. Vincent prefers painting to eating, but will also frequently miss meals (he leaves the table in a fit of anger at his brother's), or be interrupted as he eats (notably in the gratinée scene, where this is treated humorously). At one point he will ask a child for a piece of his brioche. As he lays dying, his last words are 'J'ai faim' ('I am hungry'). When Madame Ravoux sends up a bowl of soup for Vincent, Théo fears it

9 'He did not give back the money' [...] 'The wild harvest of great works was useless ... useless the quest for the ultimate secrets. The fervour was useless. Because everything is useless. Knowledge is a serpent that devours itself. What could there be beyond the field of wheat with crows? Nothing but the horrifying void to which a man can reply only with bitter silence.'

will be dangerous for him to eat it, and in a gesture emblematic of his unwillingness to 'nourish' his brother with the esteem and approval he merits, Théo will consume it himself.

Given the extraordinary importance of Théo in Van Gogh's life, women might be expected to play a relatively limited role in Pialat's account of the last months of the painter's career. However, Pialat anchors Van Gogh's tragedy in a series of failed relationships with women: with his new sister-in-law Jo, who alienates him from Théo; with Marguerite Gachet (although there is no historical evidence to support a romantic relationship between them) and with Cathy, identified as the prostitute to whom he sent his severed ear. In Pialat's version of Van Gogh's story, it is a crucial relationship between money, art and women that leads to the artist's death. This recalls the romantic paradigm analysed by Geneviève Sellier in New Wave films, a paradigm based on the portrayal of women in romantic literature, in which women and domesticity become the ultimate threat to an artist's creative autonomy and *his* (only men are artists) very existence (Sellier 2000: 747) Some elements of the paradigm surface in the film, notably the association of women with daily routine, nature and reproduction, which makes them inimical to the spiritual transforma-tions of art: 'Les femmes, il n'y a que la matière qui les intéresse' ('Women, only the material interests them'), Vincent remarks wryly to Dr Gachet when his work on Marguerite's portrait is interrupted by a call to join the others at lunch. However, if women do draw Vincent away from painting, they also provide a measure of companionship and acceptance that makes it possible for him, for a time, to continue to paint.

By contrast, the primary male characters, Théo and Dr Gachet, reinforce his sense of alienation. Théo withholds his approval and Dr Gachet appears to use his relationship with his patient to strengthen his ties to Paris art circles and enhance both his own reputation and his art collection. Pialat makes Gachet the most unsympathetic character in the film, fawning and unctuous, a stand-in (with Théo) for the bourgeois art establishment, a name-dropper and a hypocrite. Incapable of valuing true originality, his collection of works by contemporary artists is less a sign of his taste or connoisseurship than a form of snobbism and an extension of bourgeois notions of property. Pialat's Vincent despises men like Gachet, to the point where the artist, on his deathbed, will actually slap him.

Pialat's film then moves away from the old romantic paradigm – in which women threaten the artist's survival – towards a new economy in which the artist is identified with women in his need to be connected to the larger collectivity, now redefined as both a public and a market, in order to survive. The artist then assumes an ambiguous gender status which is brought home most clearly in *Van Gogh* by the relationship between Vincent and Marguerite. In fact, it is Marguerite's revolt against her father and his conventional ideas about how women should behave that initially draws her to Vincent. When she complains that she is not allowed to speak freely and is forced to find an outlet for her emotions in embroidery, Vincent counters with 'Ma peinture c'est un peu ma broderie' ('Painting is my form of embroidery'). The remark establishes a parallel between them, which is reinforced when Gachet angrily accuses Marguerite of being hysterical when she declares her love for Vincent. However, it is Jo who underlines the social equivalent of Vincent's diminished market value when she observes maliciously to Théo that the doctor would have welcomed Vincent as a suitor for Marguerite if he were a successful painter. The same calculation of market value occurs later when Suzanne Valadon approaches Théo to ask him to sell her work. He dismisses her by claiming she has made a reputation as a model and that no one will be interested in her paintings. Although as Vincent remarked wryly when Suzanne announced that she had started to paint : 'Tout le monde peint maintenant, même les femmes' ('Everyone paints now, even women').

Pialat's Vincent will ultimately commit suicide, not because he understands, or fails to understand, some ultimate truth about art, or because he sacrifices his creative autonomy for the love of a woman, but because – unlike even the village idiot whose portrait he paints in the film – he has been unable to earn a place in society. His paintings have no market value because Vincent fails to please bourgeois tastes; even Marguerite rejects her portrait claiming Vincent has painted her dress a hideous mauve and made her hands look like claws – although her father will keep the painting for his collection. Because Vincent's art has no value as an object of exchange, his paintings are reduced to the status of material objects. They become a physical encumbrance, an ever increasing accumulation of canvases which gradually fill all of the available storage space in Théo's Paris apartment and crowd into the Ravoux's spare room. By contrast, Vincent's own status increasingly diminishes, even in his own estimation. He tells Théo that his recent production, including his portrait of Marguerite, is worthless. His diminished status becomes even clearer when Cathy, the prostitute, refuses to let Vincent touch her when she can choose between him and more respectable (and better-paying) bourgeois clients like his brother.

In Pialat's version of Vincent's martyrdom – a version that reflects his anger over his own financial difficulties, his delayed recognition as a filmmaker who might otherwise have been part of the New Wave, and his allegiance to the working class – it is a society made up of men like Gachet who will kill art and who ultimately make Vincent's death inevitable. Appropriately then, it is Gachet who pronounces Vincent's death sentence, even before he has actually died, by breaking the news to Théo that nothing can be done for his brother. Pialat's film portrays what amounts to a kind of heroic last stand at Auvers, where Vincent produces painting after painting in an exhausting and vain effort to fight for a place in society. Pialat asks us to measure his suicide against the heroism of doomed soldiers in the Commune, which is evoked in the film through a touchingly halting rendition of a love song that was subsequently associated with the massacre of the spring and summer of 1871: 'Le Temps des cerises'.

The dramatic value of Vincent's death is as diminished as his value in the art market, where a lack of recognition dooms his paintings: he merely turns his back to the world, his face towards the wall of his room and dies. His death does not even take place on camera, but is announced after the fact by Théo. Pialat leaves it to the women in the film to give expression to the painter's passing and to mourn. The real drama that concludes the film is not Vincent's death, but Madame Ravoux' accident. Her scream when a trapdoor drops on her foot functions as a displaced expression of Vincent's agony. The relative importance attached to the two events becomes both a terrible indictment of society and an ironic commentary on the fact that life goes on.

Style and form

One of the most striking visual features of Pialat's film is the way it substitutes its own images both for Van Gogh's work and that of artists now considered some of the great masters of the nineteenth century: Renoir, Monet, Pissarro, Degas, suggesting the kind of lighting and compositions we have learned to see through the lens of their paintings. There are boats on the Oise, rows of poplars in the countryside, bathers at the river, a sun-dappled lunch in a garden, dancing in a *guingette*, or open-air café; Théo's wife Jo bathing in a metal tub, an absinthe drinker, dancers doing the cancan, and the wheatfields of Van Gogh's final paintings. The artful but naturalised images of the film replace the paintings, as though, too much a part of the artist's legend, it were pointless to show them. There is a deceptive sense that Pialat is removing the picture frame that separates life from fine art in an attempt to restore art's more human dimension – this paralleling his attempt to portray Van Gogh as just a man who works at painting – as Vincent says in the film – 'simplement, et à ma propre façon' ('simply and in my own way').

This has its counterpart in the nostalgia for a truly popular art fed by Pialat's memories of the audience's enjoyment of the Saturday night movies he attended in his adolescence. In *Van Gogh* this takes the form of an interest in public performance, particularly singing and dancing. Two important extended sequences – the luncheon at Gachet's, followed by a walk along the river to a *guingette*, where the adults, if not Marguerite, will dance; and the cabaret scenes, complete with a frenzied cancan, where she will dance for the first time – emphasise this kind of popular performance.

The two dance sequences are formal opposites, one outdoors and sunlit, the other nocturnal, but filmed indoors; one ending in a reaffirmation of family unity despite underlying tensions that provoke Vincent's mock suicide; the other providing an illusory moment of community – a microcosm of the artist's social world – that will leave Van Gogh with a profound sense of isolation that culminates in his death. Both illustrate an aspect of the film's major theme (and one of the major themes in Pialat's work) the place of the individual in the collectivity. Here, as in *Police*, Pialat moves in more closely to his actors. There are two notable lingering close-ups of Vincent: the first showing his reaction as he recognises Marguerite at the cabaret and realises she has run away to meet him; a second in the train back to Auvers when he retreats from Marguerite into a solitude that she does not understand. However, by and large, Pialat continues to favour long and medium-long shots that link his characters to their environment rather than close-ups that isolate them.

The first of the two extended sequences, the luncheon at Dr Gachet's, takes place outdoors in the garden where Gachet, Jo and Théo, Marguerite and Vincent are gathered around the table, although the meal is already over. Mme Chevalier and Adeline Ravoux settle at the table with the guests. The congenial atmosphere recalls the sense of community at the outdoor picnic in *Loulou* and inspires Vincent (aided by Théo) to stage a ribald presentation in which he dresses up as Toulouse-Lautrec. This will be followed by Gachet, acting out the roles of Quasimodo, a camel and a witch, all to general hilarity. When Marguerite embarrassedly refuses Vincent's request for a poem, Théo proposes a song. Pialat will frame the four women, of different classes and at different stages in their lives, in a single shot as they sing the first stanza of *Le Temps des cerises*. The song becomes a homage to spring, young love and the song of the 'merle moqueur' (mocking blackbird) whose whistling is superior to human music-making. In fact, one of the underlying themes of the film, paradoxically, given its subject, is the beauty and complexity of nature, and its superiority to 'art'.

If the subsequent walk along the Oise breaks the mood, and emphasises the differences that separate the various members of the group, they will be reintegrated in the community of the *guinguette* where piano and accordion will draw almost everyone into the dance – even Cathy will whirl out of the crowd to pull Vincent away as her partner. The dancing stops only briefly when Dr Gachet attempts to flatter Marguerite's piano teacher by inviting her to perform Lakmé's 'L'air des clochettes'. Her self-conscious rendition of the bravura piece from Lakmé's then popular opera is implicitly contrasted with the heartfelt simplicity of the earlier singing, as 'art' perhaps more in line with bourgeois tastes. The pause in the dancing does not change the buoyant mood, but these moments of community also mask deeper concerns: Jo will in fact confide to Vincent during the walk back to the Gachets' that Théo has changed since their marriage and she fears he is unfaithful. Vincent's efforts to reassure her lead him to say that he must do something to change their situation, and he abruptly walks down to the river and throws himself in the water. This prefiguration of his suicide is dismissed as a joke by Théo, who claims that Vincent used to terrify their mother with similar stunts. However, the sense of community fades as Coco, Gachet's son, closes the gate behind their departing guests.

The parallel cabaret sequence provides a different kind of community, a marginal one in relation to the 'respectable' family community portrayed earlier, but still an alternative family that provides a refuge for Vincent after a serious argument with Théo. Ultimately he will be joined by Marguerite (escorted by Théo) who has come to Paris in search of him. In a reversal of positions that underscores the parallel Pialat establishes between Vincent and Marguérite, she will be marginalised as outsider, a naive and virginal bourgeoise. The cabaret sequence runs some twenty minutes, alternating three imposing dance segments with more intimate interactions, but as Vincent Amiel points out, none of the actions is developed, used to build a dramatic structure or establish a continuing story line (Amiel 2001: 106). The dances themselves also form discrete units with different rhythms. The first dance is Marguerite's first dance, a romantic waltz that brings her together with Vincent. The kiss they exchange as they dance prefigures their lovemaking during the final moments of the sequence – when the rest of the company launches into a wild cancan. The midpoint of the sequence is marked by Vincent's request that the accordion player sing *La Butte rouge*. The song's lyrics might be associated with the Commune (although the song actually dates from the First World War) as they celebrate heroic fighting to hold a hill, the battleground later replanted as a vineyard which transmutes the heroes' blood into wine. This performance stops the dancing and talking, bringing everyone together to listen or to accompany the singer. Vincent himself sings along in a barely audible voice with his arms around Marguerite. This celebration of 'communion' is followed by the central dance, 'La Marche', a quasi-military line-up of the entire company, marching two by two. This dance brings a form of reconciliation between the two brothers as Théo deliberately seeks out Vincent to make sure that he and Marguerite join the line of dancers with him and Cathy (although he remains unaware that he has usurped his brother's usual partner). Filmed frontally, the performers move, couple by couple, to the front of the line, then curtsey. Preternaturally solemn, they execute a series of complicated manoeuvres that contrast with the final cancan where individual dancers express their exuberance in cartwheels. This and the other dance sequences inevitably ask to be measured against the twenty-minute cancan sequence which ends Renoir's *French Cancan*. However, the energy and vitality of Renoir's film derives from a sense that the artifices of theatre heighten or intensify the 'real', while in Pialat's film the dance stages the creation of an artificial community that will disband when the night is over. When Suzanne Valadon wakes Théo early the next morning, he will leave alone. The beginning of the next sequence shows the breakdown of the relationship between Marguerite and Vincent when he abruptly moves away to a seat by himself in the empty train car that takes them back to Auvers in the early morning hours.

The picnic sequence owes some of its gaiety and beauty to the loveliness of the natural surroundings, but the second sequence reflects the artificiality and illusions of art, despite the heroic sacrifice honoured in the 'communion' of *La Butte rouge*. This suggests an underlying ambivalence about art that Pialat expressed more clearly during an interview with the review *Cinématographe* in the 1980s. He insisted that art was always inferior to life – 'Je regardais un doigt l'autre jour, et je me disais: qu'est-ce qu'une œuvre d'art à côté d' un doigt ... pourtant ça n'est rien: des tissus, un réseau très simple et très complexe de vaisseaux'[10] (Pialat 1980: 9).

Nonetheless, Joël Magny considered *Van Gogh* Pialat's master-piece, a radically new vision of the legendary painter (Magny 1992: 110). In Magny's view, Pialat successfully stripped away the hagio-graphy and the legend to represent Van Gogh as he was for his contemporaries, a man who could not have conceived that he would become a symbol of tormented and misunderstood genius – and could not have imagined his paintings would be widely popular yet valued as great art. However, the film is also subject to a second kind of reading. Vincent Amiel has argued that the structure of Pialat's film, its careful yet undifferentiated attention to events, its gaps and displacements, calls attention to the impossibility of giving a strictly realist vision of its subject. From this perspective Pialat's use of montage attempts to compensate for the limitations of film as a realist medium inherited from Lumière – whose *Arrival of a train at La Ciotat* is evoked in the first frames of the film – and its inability to convey the profound emotions that shape a vision of reality (Amiel 2001: 108). Neither reading fully accounts for Pialat's representation of his subject, although *Van Gogh* inevitably tempted Pialat to test the

10 'I was looking at my finger the other day, and I said to myself: what is a work of art in comparison with a finger ... and yet it isn't anything: some tissue, a very simple and very complex network of vessels.'

limits of his medium, measuring the art of the filmmaker against that of the expressionist painter.

Afterward

Pialat's *Van Gogh*, and Jacques Rivette's *La Belle Noiseuse*, also about a painter, if a fictional one (Balzac's Frenhofer in *Le chef d'œuvre inconnue*), represented France at the Cannes Film Festival in May of 1991. While *La Belle Noiseuse* would be named best film, there was no official recognition of *Van Gogh*. Later at the Césars, only Jacques Dutronc would win an award for his work, although *Van Gogh* was nominated in twelve different categories. In an interview with *Positif*, Pialat spoke about the film as though it were a failure and had to be reminded that the film had attracted a remarkable number of viewers, over one million four hundred thousand (Pialat 1992: 108). Yet Pialat remained dissatisfied because the most popular film of the year, *Tous les matins du monde*, a period film about a musician, brought in over two million. Pialat perhaps took this as a rejection (Mérigeau 2002: 313–14), certainly he withdrew after the film was completed, but it is equally possible that the birth of his son had more to do with the four year hiatus that separated *Van Gogh* from what would be his last film, *Le Garçu*.

References

Amiel, Vincent (2001), *Esthétique du montage*, Paris, Nathan.
Bernanos, Georges ([1926]; 1961), *Œuvres romanesques*, Paris, Gallimard.
Chevassu, François (1990), 'Les Drôles de chemins de Maurice Pialat, entretien', *Revue du cinéma*, no. 466.
Durier, Bruno (1991), '*Sous le soleil de Satan*, de Bernanos à Maurice Pialat ou d'une écriture à l'autre', *Etudes bernanosiennes* 20.
Estève, Michel (1987), *Georges Bernanos, un triple itinéraire*, Paris, Minard.
Estève, Michel (1991), '*Sous le soleil de Satan* du roman au film: note sur le surnaturel et le démoniaque' *Etudes bernanosiennes* 20.
Joyard, Olivier and Jérôme Larcher (2000), 'La Trace Dutronc', *Cahiers du cinéma*, no. 551.
Lenne, Gérard (1987), 'Critiques dans l'auditorium: perplexes', *Revue du cinéma*, no. 430.
Magny, Joël (1992), *Maurice Pialat*, Paris, Cahiers du cinéma.

Mérigeau, Pascal (2002), *Pialat*, Paris, Editions Grasset & Fasquelle.

Phillipon, Alain (1987), 'Description d'un combat', *Cahiers du cinéma*, no.399.

Perruchot, Henri (1955), *La Vie de Van Gogh*, Paris, Hachette.

Pialat, Maurice (1980), 'Entretien', *Cinématographe*, no. 57.

Pialat, Maurice (1987), 'La Ligne droite, entretien', *Cahiers du cinéma*, no. 399.

Pialat, Maurice (1992), 'Un cinéma à champ large, entretien', *Positif*, nos. 375–6.

Pialat, Maurice (2000), 'Entretien: sur la colère', *Cahiers du cinéma*, no. 550.

Powrie, Phil (1997), *French Cinema in the 1980s: Nostalgia and the Crisis of Masculinity*, Oxford, Oxford University Press.

Sellier, Geneviève (2000), 'Masculinity and Politics in the New Wave', *Sites*, vol. 4 no. 1.

Toubiana, Serge (1987), 'Editorial: Cannes, le cinéma en otage', *Cahiers du cinéma*, no. 397.

7

Conclusion: paternity and *Le Garçu*

Le Garçu, which came out in 1995, became Pialat's last film. He remained dissatisfied with it and even made plans to re-edit it, although his failing health made this one of the many projects he was not to complete. Yet *Le Garçu* is not an inappropriate conclusion to Pialat's lifework in film. It brings his career full circle, reconnecting with the autobiographical and documentary inspiration of his first films and focusing more directly on what had always been the central concern of his cinema: the family. Although the isolation of the exceptional individual had preoccupied him in *Sous le soleil de Satan* and *Van Gogh*, with *Le Garçu* Pialat returned to universal human experience: the birth of a child, the difficulty of living as a couple, the impact of the death of a parent. The film's main character is ostensibly Pialat's four-year-old son Antoine, whose voice is heard during the opening credits, however the film actually spans a lifetime (juxtaposing images of childhood with the preoccupations of middle and old age) and becomes a complex family portrait that links three generations.

The fact that the film opens with a scene in which Antoine is the central presence re-emphasises the importance Pialat accorded children, both as creations far superior to artistic productions (the superiority of life to art had been an underlying theme in *Van Gogh*) – and as a measure of the family and the society in which they will have to find a place. The crying child of Pialat's first short documentary *L'amour existe* already suggested a concern for children that reflected both Pialat's memories of his own childhood, and his desire to be a father. He claimed that his decision to treat the problem of adoption in his first full-length film, *L'Enfance nue*, was influenced by the fact he was childless (Pialat 1980: 4) and after playing the father in *A nos amours*, he speculated that something was lacking in his life, both as a man and as an artist, because he had no children:

> J'ai lu, et je serais assez tenté de croire, que la paternité est plus nécessaire psychologiquement à l'homme que la maternité à la femme. Et pourtant, j'ai aussi tendance à croire que l'homme a une vie finie qui se résume plutôt à lui, contrairement à la femme qui est la génération et la reproduction. Je suis tiraillé. Je suis sûr qu'il y a une insuffisance dans ma vie tout court, et puis dans cette vie d'un type qui prétend faire des films. Des circonstances dans ma vie ont fait que je n'ai pas eu d'enfant, après c'est devenu une chose très compliquée ... Je devrais peut-être tout faire pour en avoir, y compris en adopter un ... il y a assez de mômes malheureux dans le monde ...C'est ce constant duel entre la vie pour soi et la vie dont on sait qu'elle n'existe que parce qu'il y a un enchaînement, et la mort.[1] (Pialat 1983: 17–18)

Perhaps a similar duel between the artist and the father explains Pialat's decision to memorialise the birth of his son by creating a full-length 'fictional' film. Yet the film also shares a good deal with the genre of the home movie – and it was filmed in Pialat's home territory, if not his home (with the exception of the sequence filmed on Mauritius island – although its French name, 'l'île Maurice', suggests a connection). Two sequences, including the final one, were set in his favourite Paris restaurant, 'Le Scampi' (Mérigeau 2002: 331). More importantly, however, the film brings together members of Pialat's cinematic and immediate family, blurring the distinctions between reality and fiction. The four-year-old Antoine was merely himself, while in taking the role of Antoine's father, Gérard Depardieu remained 'Gérard'. Antoine clearly recognises him as a close family friend he calls 'le gros Gégé' (big Gégé). However, as 'Gérard Gardy' (the fictional surname taken from a character in *La Maison des bois*),

---

1 'I have read, and I am tempted to believe, that paternity is more necessary to men than maternity to women. And yet, I also tend to believe that men have a finite life that is summed up in themselves, unlike women who are generation and reproduction. I'm torn. I am sure there is something missing in my life, and also in my life as a guy who claims he makes films. Circumstances in my life have led to my not having a child and since, it has become very complicated ... Perhaps I should do everything I could to have one, including adopting one ... there are enough unhappy kids in the world. There's this constant duel between life for itself and life that ... only exists because there is a connection with others, and death.'

Depardieu also played a character based on Pialat's experience as a pharmaceutical representative and a salesman for Olivetti. Elizabeth Depardieu assumed the role of Gérard's first wife, her name, 'Micheline' making explicit the reference to Pialat's autobiography and connecting the fictional wife to two real couples.

As in a home movie, accidents and mistakes, including Antoine's unpredictable reactions, provide touching and amusing moments. Antoine's frequent glances toward the camera reveal his awareness of the presence of one or another of his parents – and of the film crew. Pialat does not efface the presence of the camera; the viewer can see reflections of the film crew in the windows of the bus that Antoine and his mother board on the island, while the local children who appear to react with delight to the passage of the bus are in fact reacting to the filming. Nor did Pialat see any need to dub the sequence in which Dominique Rocheteau – the well-known soccer player – misspoke and referred to Sylvie, Antoine's mother, although Sylvie Danton Pialat never makes an appearance, and there is no such character in the film.

Although Géraldine Pailhas's character, Sophie, substitutes for Antoine's real mother, Sylvie Pialat remains powerfully present, if invisible, in the film. In fact, in the opening sequence between Antoine and 'Sophie', it was Sylvie Danton who played opposite her son. Pialat merely used a series of shot/counter shots to edit Pailhas into the film, substituting the actress for the real mother (Pailhas 2003: 52). However, if there is only one mother in the film, Pialat multiplies the number of fathers. There is Antoine's biological father, Gérard, but also Jeannot, Antoine's mother's partner, who becomes a substitute father, as well as Gérard's father, '*le garçu*', whose nickname gives the film its title. Pialat's use of this *auvergnat* patois goes back to *Nous ne vieillirons pas ensemble* where Jean mumbled '*le garçu*' as he greeted his father and the father in *La Gueule ouverte* was also referred to as *le garçu*. However, the absence of any explanation of the word until well into *Le Garçu* may lead the viewer to think it refers to '*le garçon*', the boy Antoine, particularly as Antoine is introduced in the initial sequence. Instead, the nickname derives from Gérard's (and presumably Pialat's) father's habit of referring to himself as 'his father's son', the usage emphasising both the continuity between generations and the father's importance in establishing a child's identity. However, the curious confusion between the father and the son created by the title also recalls the difficulties experienced by the adult male characters in Pialat's films who remain sons rather than becoming fathers.

Le Garçu represents an important shift in this paradigm as Gérard is both a son and a father; he and Sophie are the only couple in Pialat's cinematic universe who actually produce a child and become a family. Yet the film chronicles the couple's break-up, although, typically, the highly fragmented narrative provides no clear motive for it. The tension between Sophie and Gérard is already evident from Gérard's cautious embrace in their first scene together. Certainly Gérard's travels and preoccupation with business, his episodic presence at home and his attentions to other women fuel Sophie's unhappiness and resentment – and link his character to the straying or absent fathers of *L'Enfance nue* and *La Gueule ouverte*. Nonetheless, when present, he is an adoring – if not selfless – father, as jealous of his son's attention and affection as a lover, and sometimes hurt by the child's short attention span or changes in mood. Twice the film shows him watching or lying next to the sleeping Antoine, caressing his hand or arm. By contrast, Gérard roughly shakes Sophie awake when the two of them are alone together in a hotel room, telling her he cannot bear her snoring.

After he and Sophie have separated, Sophie will establish a relationship with Jeannot, a former acquaintance and business associate of Gerard's. Jeannot will ultimately move in with Sophie and Antoine, inevitably distancing Gérard from his son. Gérard begins to haunt the entrance to Antoine's kindergarten, hoping to get a glimpse of him. As this suggests, the crucial emotional and family connections in Pialat's film are between fathers and sons, despite the proliferation of female characters around Gérard – a pattern that echoes the construction of *Van Gogh*. Gérard is in fact surrounded by Micheline, Sophie and Cathy, his occasional mistress, all of whom remain emotionally attached to him. However, the film fails to explore the dramatic possibilities of their relationships even when they hint at other complicated family stories, such as Cathy's confession that her former husband physically abused her. Micheline in particular remains a mysterious character, her connection to Gérard never made explicit, merely summed up in a name that would have meant nothing to a viewer ignorant of Pialat's autobiography. Ultimately this matters little, however, because the crucial love triangle in the film is created by Gérard's rivalry with Jeannot for the role of primary male figure in Antoine's life.

Gérard's jealousy is made clear in the sequence where he runs into Jeannot and Antoine outside a café and finds that Antoine pays him only cursory attention, more interested in playing pinball with Jeannot. When 'rejected', Gérard leaves abruptly, although he pauses just before he pulls away on his motorcycle to try to catch his son's attention, calling his name as he watches him through the large plate-glass window of the café. After this failure, Gérard dramatically recaptures his son's attention in the next sequence, one of the most striking in the film. He rouses Jeannot and Sophie by barging into the apartment at three o'clock in the morning carrying a child-sized electric car tied up with a large bow. Antoine is besides himself and Sophie is forced to capitulate despite her initial disapproval, watching half-indulgently with Jeannot as Gérard shows Antoine how to drive his present around and around the apartment. Then, the first flush of excitement passed, Gérard takes his leave, blowing kisses to Antoine.

Gérard's intensity and drama, his restlessness and quick irritability, match the narrative structure of relatively short self-contained sequences which are animated, even literally driven, primarily by his presence. This structure reflects the real circumstances of the filming: Pialat's own poor health and the fact that he tired easily, as well as the necessity of working with a child whose concentration and attention span were limited. Yet Pialat also uses the film's structure to establish a parallel between the son and his immature father which becomes clear in a brief sequence where the two play together and watch videos. Gérard becomes edgy and irritable to the degree that Antoine, in a disarming role reversal, rebukes him.

This film, like most of Pialat's films, unfolds as a succession of present moments, fragments of a story that lacks a conventional dramatic focus. However, the sequences have a more 'painterly' function, rather like individual brushstrokes, patches of colour or variations on a form whose repetitions forge connections and ultimately create the composition. The various iterations of the father–son relationship unify the composition, becoming the thematic equivalent of a pictorial motif. The story of *le garçu* and his own father then becomes crucial to Pialat's portrayal of paternity. By going back two generations Pialat restores family connections that were broken by death but which have been given renewed significance with the birth of Antoine. The film then also provides a frame for retelling important family stories: Pialat has Gérard retell the story of his own grandfather's death in an accident just before he was born (preserving the memory for his son and for posterity) and also finishes the work of mourning begun with *La Gueule ouverte*. On a formal level, the sequence also provides the opportunity, one Pialat had long desired, to redo *La Gueule ouverte* by representing the death of a parent in a way that would touch rather than repel the viewer.

The *garçu*'s death brings Gérard back to the region in which his father grew up and where his father's family had a long history. Yet the beauty of the autumn landscape also increases Gérard's anguish by bringing home the recognition that he does not really know the country, and in some profound sense he did not know his father. 'Finalement je n'ai jamais connu mon pays. Jamais plus je ne reviendrai' ('In the end, I never really knew this country. I will never come back'), he tells Sophie, who has accompanied him. Before they leave for Paris they stop briefly to greet family friends, but barely get out of the car. The *garçu*'s death reveals the depth of Gérard's alienation and intensifies his sense that he is not at home anywhere. Although the constant travelling required for his work reinforces this sense of rootlessness, Gérard's lack of connection to his father's world also suggests that, unlike his father, he would more readily identify himself as 'his son's father', than as 'his father's son'.

This is precisely what is at issue during a key scene near the end of the film, when Gérard wanders into Sophie's apartment as her groceries are being delivered, finding Jeannot in the kitchen. It has been three weeks since Gérard has made an appearance and he is formally dressed in a suit, clearly having dropped in on his way somewhere else. 'J'arrive et je repars' ('I've just come and I'm leaving') he tells Sophie. He complains about Sophie's choice of groceries, then questions Sophie about Antoine's activities, unhappy that he cannot see the boy, who happens to be spending the night with a friend. He is disconcerted and not particularly pleased to discover that Antoine will begin a half-day at school very soon. His constant needling irks Jeannot, usually quiet and even-tempered, who takes him to task for failing to spend time with his son. Taken aback, Gérard blames his long absences on the pace of his business, saying that he does what he can, concluding: 'mais je peux te dire une chose, c'est que je suis sûr qu'Antoine sait que je suis son père' ('I can tell you one thing and that's that I'm sure Antoine knows I'm his father). While there is no reason to doubt what Jeannot's rather dry 'Ça c'est sûr'('that's for sure') confirms, the film does not suggest that Antoine shows any real preference for his father. Moreover, as Luc Moullet points out, the penultimate scene of the film, which follows Antoine's kindergarten group to the park, visually connects the greens and golds of the autumn landscape to the countryside in Auvergne, as though a love of the land had skipped a generation, connecting the boy more closely with his paternal grandfather (Moullet 1996: 49).

The final sequence provides an emblematic representation of the father's isolation, and his painful separation from the family that might have anchored his own life. Gérard, alone, walking down the street in the evening, is hailed by a passing car. It is Sophie, with Antoine in the back seat. She is surprised to see him, perhaps surprised that he is in town, and he gets in with them. Although it is late he has not had dinner and they go to his favourite restaurant. The owner, a friend of Gérard's, entertains Antoine by letting him watch as he feeds ham into a slicing machine. When Sophie expresses concern that the machine is dangerous, Gérard leaves their table to make sure all is well. He then goes outside, looking in at Antoine through the window in a repetition of the earlier café scene. Here he flattens his face up against the glass, moving his mouth to indicate he is hungry, then pretends to eat the slice of ham that Antoine laughingly offers him from the other side of the glass. This image is the last in a long series of moments during the film when Gérard lovingly and 'hungrily' watches his son, but remains distanced from him, separated from Antoine as much by his work, his absence from the family circle, and his own unhappiness and resentment, as by the plate-glass window. When he rejoins Sophie, Gérard does not sit down next to her but closer to the edge of the frame, as though he were about to drift out of the picture. Then the camera pans to Sophie, suddenly tearful, as she dabs at her eyes with the white table napkin.

In a sense, the film does not so much tell a story as register the psychic state of the family, particularly that of the father, who, no longer a son, will now never fully assume the role of the father. The family members are separated from one another, even within the same space. Sophie's moment of tearful solitude in the final image sums up the situation, her unexplained tears becoming a formal expression of what each of them has lost. Yet, ultimately, the film shows Gérard to be the most isolated, having lost his father, and to some degree his son, while an earlier scene with Cathy in which he gasps for breath after they make love prefigures his death.

The sadness of the ending, coupled with the anger and ambivalence that underlie many of the characters' exchanges, may explain the film's lack of commercial success despite some extraordinary sequences with Antoine. Nonetheless, *Le Garçu* is a powerful and unsettling portrayal of the nuclear family in the 1990s; one that emphasises both gender conflict, and the difficult and problematic role of the father at a time when the father's presence is no longer strictly necessary, either for procreation or to give the child a name. Yet Pialat refused to let the father die in *A nos amours*, and the figure of the father remains crucial to his cinema. Nor should the pervasive sadness of *Le Garçu* disguise the fact that in his final film Pialat refused to abandon the family. Sophie has in fact established a successful relationship with Jeannot, who is a constant and stable presence both in her life and that of Antoine. This explains Sophie's greater serenity and willingness to accept Gérard as he is – without being wounded either by his constant absences or his hostility – and to allow him to remain an important presence in Antoine's life. No longer the nineteenth-century head of household, the standard-bearer of traditional values, the protector of defenceless women and children, or even the head of the family business, Gérard remains his son's father, despite his absence from the family circle. The film elides the fact that his presence in his son's life would be much more problematic without Sophie's acceptance of his role.

The overwhelming importance Pialat accords paternity shapes his attitude towards his work and his sense of cinematic authorship. It emerges in his insistence on being involved in writing or rewriting his scenarios, or his effort to infuse his films with autobiographical elements that would make each of them a disguised or displaced autobiography. Yet his identification with masculine characters who are primarily sons, or who, like his character in *A nos amours*, abandon the family, reinforces his link to the *Nouvelle Vague*. Their 'oedipal' rebellion against the history and tradition represented by the *cinéma de papa* is not fully assumed in Pialat's cinema, but takes the form of an estrangement or alienation. This is reflected both in his view of himself as a marginal, and marginalised, filmmaker and his unwillingness to ally himself either with the fathers or the sons.

Pialat's hostility toward the successful 'sons' of the New Wave was no secret, but his admiration for the 'fathers': Renoir, Carné, Lang or Bresson, even Ford, was rarely unqualified. When he admitted to a passion for Dreyer in his last interview with *Cahiers du cinéma* he was quick to add that he 'used to' have a passion for Dreyer, but that he disliked seeing people sanctified because it was a sign of academism (Pialat 2000: 59). He clearly feared the approbation of the 'academy' as much as he desired it, believing, on some level at least, that official recognition would be a sign his work had lost both its freshness and its edge. This emerges in his dismissal of *Sous le soleil de Satan* as an academic film despite his great personal investment in it (Pialat 2000: 59). When *Cahiers du cinéma* reminded him that a number of young filmmakers saw him as a major influence on their work, he seemingly drew little satisfaction from this, reminding his interviewer that 'Lorsqu'on considère quelqu'un, lorsqu'on l'admire, c'est toujours à double tranchant: c'est le père et il faut tuer le père'[2] (Pialat 2000: 58).

Yet *Le Garçu* suggests a greater willingness to overlook the son's potential to become a dangerous rival in order to value him as the father's legacy. Something similar emerges during Pialat's last interview with *Cahiers* when he discusses a scene from Bresson's *Journal d'un curé de campagne* in which, as Pialat describes it, the priest is packing, putting a number of seemingly insignificant objects into a basket. Pialat expressed amazement that Bresson would waste time on such a scene, claiming it was merely a way to fill an otherwise empty moment, adding: 'C'est dommage que je n'aie pas été prof à la Femis, je leur aurais appris peut-être quelques trucs, je pourrais faire des cours là-dessus. Je montrerais la scène de Bresson. On en a besoin'[3] (Pialat 2000: 61). Pialat's desire to shape a younger generation of filmmakers suggests a shift that is reflected in *Le Garçu*, where the son becomes a father and moves beyond his own story to take his place in a larger family history.

2 'When you have consideration for someone, when you admire him, it always cuts two ways: he's the father and you have to kill the father.'

3 'It's too bad that I haven't been a teacher at the Femis [La Fédération européenne des métiers de l'image et du son: the national film school], I would perhaps have taught them a thing or two, I could do courses on this. I would show the scene from Bresson. They need it.'

References

Mérigeau, Pascal (2002), *Pialat*, Paris, Editions Grasset & Fasquelle.

Moullet, Luc (1996), 'La palette à Pialat', *Cahiers du cinéma*, no. 498.

Pailhas, Géraldine (2003), 'Témoignages', *Cahiers du cinéma*, no. 576.

Pialat, Maurice (1980), 'Entretien', *Cinématographe*, no. 57.

Pialat, Maurice (1983), 'Entretien', *Cinématographe*, no. 94.

Pialat, Maurice (1984), *A nos amours: scénario et dialogue du film*, Paris, L'Herminier.

Pialat, Maurice (2000) 'Entretien: sur la colère', *Cahiers du cinéma*, no. 550.

Filmography

In addition to direct sources, this filmography draws on earlier work by Joël Magny (*Maurice Pialat* 1992), Toffetti and Tassone, curators (*Maurice Pialat, enfant sauvage* 1992) and Pascal Mérigeau (*Pialat* 2002).

Pialat as actor

Les Veuves de 15 ans (1954), dir. Jean Rouch
Le Jeu de la nuit (1957), dir. Daniel Costelle
Que la bête meure (1969), dir. Claude Chabrol
Mes petites amoureuses (1974), dir. Jean Eustache
Les Lolos de Lola (1974), dir. Bernard Dubois
Grosse (1985), dir. Brigitte Rohan

Short films (amateur)

Isabelle aux Dombes 1951
Riviera di Brenta 1952
Congrès Eucharistique diocésain 1953
Drôles de bobines 1957, 15 min.
L'Ombre familière 1958, 20 mins.
   Principal actors: Sophie Marin, Jacques Portet

Short films (professional)

L'Amour existe (*Love Exists*), 1961 , 21 mins, b/w

Production: Films de la Pléiade (Pierre Braunberger)
Script: Maurice Pialat
Photography: Gilbert Sarthre
Music: Georges Delerue
Voice-over: Jean-Loup Reinhold
Editing: Kenout Peltier
Awards: Prix Louis Lumière 1961; Lion at the Venice Film Festival 1961

Janine, 1962, 16 mins, b/w

Production: France Opera Films
Assistant director: Gabriel Garran
Script: Claude Berri
Photography: Jean-Marc Ripert
Editing: Geneviève Bastid
Sound: Bernard Meusnier
Music: René Urtreger
Principal actors: Hubert Deschamps (Hubert), Claude Berri (Claude), Evelyne Ker (Janine), Mouflette (Lili)

Jardins d'Arabie, 1963, 23 mins, col.

Production: Tony Adès
Photography: Gilbert Sarthre

Four films produced and distributed by Como Films (Samy Halfon), 1964

Photography: Willy Kurant (b/w)

Pehlivan, 13 mins, commentary by Maurice Pialat

Istanbul, 13 mins, commentary by A. Falk
Music: folk music of Turkey

Byzance, 11 mins, commentary by Stefan Zweig, read by André Reybaz
Music: period and liturgical music

Maître Galip, 11 mins, commentary by Nazim Hikmet, read by André Raybaz

Short fims made for Francophone television 1965–69

Production: Ministry of Foreign Affairs

Les Champs Elysées

Pigalle

L'Usine marémotrice de la Rance

Anvers

La Parisienne et les grands magasins

Agnès Varda tourne

La Camargue

Marseille

Villages d'enfants, 1969, (Children's Villages—shelters for abused or abandoned children), 16 mm, 40 mins, col.

Production: Mouvement des villages d'enfants
Photography: Jean-Marc Ripert
Editing: Arlette Langmann, Martine Giordano

Made for television

La Maison des bois (***The House in the woods***), 1970–71, 7 episodes, 40 to 58 mins, col.

Production: ORTF, Son et Lumière
Scenario: René Wheeler, dialogues: René Wheeler and Maurice Pialat
Assistant directors: Bernard Dubois, Jean-Claude Bourlat
Photography: Roger Duculot
Editing: Arlette Langmann, Martine Giordano
Sound: Norbert Gernolle
Sets: Isabel Lapierre
Principal actors: Pierre Doris (Albert Picard), Jacqueline Dufranne (Jeanne Picard), Agathe Nathanson (Marguerite), Henri Puff (Marcel Picard), Hervé Lévy (Hervé Gardy), Michel Tarrazon (Michel Latour), Albert Martinez (Bébert), Fernand Gravey (the Marquis), Maurice Pialat (the schoolteacher), Marie-Christine Boulard (Mme Pouilly), Micha Bayard (Mme Latour), Paul Crauchet (Paul Grady), Barbara Laage (Hélène), Brigitte Perrier (Brigitte), Alexandre Rignault (Birot), Dominique Maurin (Jeannot), Yves Laumet (Bourlat), Jean Mauvais (Mahut), Henri Saulquin (the beadle)

L'enfance nue (**Naked Childhood**), 1969, 82 mins, Eastmancolour

Production: Parc Films, les Films du Carrosse (François Truffaut), Renn
Productions (Claude Berri), Parafrance Film
Executive producer: Véra Belmont
Assistant directors: Denis Epstein
Scenario: Maurice Pialat; Adaptation: Maurice Pialat, Arlette Langmann
Photography: Claude Beausoleil, Jean-Marc Ripert
Editing: Arlette Langmann
Sound: Henri Moline
Principal actors: Michel Tarrazon (François), Marie-Louise Thierry (Mme
Thierry), René Thierry (M. Thierry), Marie Marc (Mémère la vieille),
Henri Puff (Raoul), Linda Gutemberg (Simone Joigny), Raoul Billerey
(Robby Joigny), Pierrette Deplanque (Josette), Maurice Coussoneau
(Letillon, the director of Social Services), Claire Thierry (aunt Claire),
Yolande Coleau (escort for the children in transit)
Awards: Prix Jean Vigo 1969, Selected for the Venice Film Festival 1971

Nous ne vieillirons pas ensemble (**We will not grow old together**), 1972, 107 mins, Eastmancolour

Production: Lido Films, Empire Films
Assistant directors: Jean-Claude Bourlat, Daniel Imbert, Jean-Luc Millorit,
Alain Etève
Scenario: Maurice Pialat, adapted from his novel *Nous ne vieillirons pas
ensemble* (Ed. Galleria, 1972)
Photography: Luciano Tovoli
Editing: Arlette Langmann, Bernard Dubois, Corinne Lazare
Sound: Claude Jauvert
Principal actors: Marlène Jobert (Catherine), Jean Yanne (Jean), Macha Méril
(Françoise), Christine Fabréga (Catherine's mother), Jacques Galland
(Catherine's father), Muse Dalbray (Catherine's grandmother), Patricia
Pierangeli (Annie), Maurice Risch (Michel), Harry Max (Jean's father)
Awards: Best male actor to Jean Yanne, Cannes Film Festival 1972

La Gueule ouverte (**'Mouth Agape'**), 1974, 85 mins, Eastmancolour

Production: Lido Films, Films La Boétie
Scenario, adaptation: Maurice Pialat
Assistant directors: Bernard Grenet, Bernard Dubois
Photography: Nestor Almendros
Editing: Arlette Langmann, Bernard Dubois
Sound: Raymond Adam
Principal actors: Hubert Deschamps (Roger, the 'garçu'), Monique
Mélinand (Monique), Philippe Léotard (Philippe), Nathalie Baye (Nathalie)

Passe ton bac d'abord (Pass your exams first), 1979, 85 mins, Eastman-colour

Production: Films du Livradois, Renn Productions, FR3, INA
Scenario: Maurice Pialat
Assistant directors: Patrick Grandperret, Emmanuel Clot, Jean-Marie Duhard
Photography: Pierre-William Glenn, Jean-Paul Jansen
Editing: Arlette Langmann, Sophie Coussein, Martine Giordano
Sound: Pierre Gamet, Michel Laurent
Principal actors: Sabine Haudepin (Elisabeth), Philippe Marlaud (Philippe), Annick Alane (Elisabeth's mother), Michel Caron (Elisabeth's father), Christian Bouillette (proprietor of the Caron), Bernard Tronczyk, (Bernard), Patrick Lepzynski (Patrick),Valérie Chassigneux (Patrick's sister), Joséphine and François Lepzynski (Patrick's parents), Jean-François Adam (philosophy professor), Agnès Makowiak (Agnès), Charline Bourré (Charline), Patrick Playez (Rocky), Muriel Lacroix (Muriel), Frédérique Cerbonnet (Frédérique), Stanislawa Tronczyk (Bernard's mother)

Loulou, 1980, 110 mins, Eastmancolour

Production: Action Films, Gaumont.
Scenario: Arlette Langmann, dialogue: Arlette Langmann and Maurice Pialat
Assistant directors: Patrick Grandperret, Dominique Bonnaud, Pierre Wallon
Photography: Pierre-William Glenn, Jacques Loiseleux
Editing: Yann Dedet, Sophie Coussein; Assistant Editors: Pascale Granelle, Corinne Lazare, Luigi De Angelis
Sound: Dominique Dalmasso
Music: Philippe Sarde
Sets: Max Berto
Principal actors: Isabelle Huppert (Nelly), Gérard Depardieu (Loulou), Guy Marchand (André), Humbert Balsan (Michel, Nelly's brother), Bernard Tronczyk (Rémy), Xavier Saint-Macary (Bernard), Christian Boucher (Pierrot), Frédérique Cerbonnet (Dominique), Jacqueline Dufranne (Mémère), Patrick Playez (Thomas), Gérald Garnier (Lulu)

A nos amours (To those we love), 1983

Production: Films du Livradois, Gaumont, FR3
Assistant directors: Florence Quentin, Cyril Collard, Christian Argentino
Scenario: Arlette Langmann and Maurice Pialat
Photography: Jacques Loiseleux, Pierre Novion, Patrice Guillou, Christian Fournier

Editing: Yann Dedet, Sophie Coussein, Valérie Condroyer, Corinne Lazare, Jean Gargonne, Nathalie Letrosne, Catherine Legault

Sound: Jean Umansky, François de Morant, Julien Cloquet, Thierry Jeandroz

Sets: Jean-Paul Camail, Arlette Langmann

Principal actors: Sandrine Bonnaire (Suzanne), Dominique Besnehard (Robert), Maurice Pialat (Roger), Evelyne Ker (Betty), Anne-Sophie Maillé (Anne), Christophe Odent (Michel), Cyr Boitard (Luc), Maïté Maillé (Martine), Pierre-Loup Rajot (Bernard), Cyril Collard (Jean-Pierre), Nathalie Gureghian (Nathalie), Jacques Fieschi (Jacques), Caroline Cibot (Charline), Tsilka Theodorou (Fanny), Tom Stevens (the American), Valérie Schlumberger (Marie-France, Robert's wife)

Awards: Prix Louis Delluc 1983, *César* for the Best Film 1983

Police, 1985, 113 mins, Eastmancolour

Production: Gaumont, TF1

Assistant directors: Didier Creste, Jean-Luc Olivier, Michel Acerbo

Scenario: Catherine Breillat, Sylvie Danton, Jacques Fieschi, Maurice Pialat, based on an original idea developed by Catherine Breillat

Photography: Luciano Tovoli

Editing: Yann Dedet, assisted by Hélène Viard, Nathalie Letrosne

Continuity: Jacques Loiseleux

Sound: Bernard Aubouy, Laurent Poirier

Sets: Constantin Mejinski

Principal actors: Gérard Depardieu (Mangin), Sophie Marceau (Noria), Richard Anconina (Lambert), Pascale Rocard (Marie Vedret), Sandrine Bonnaire (Lydie), Frank Karoui (René), Jonathan Leina (Simon), Jacques Mathou (Gauthier), Bernard Fuzellier (suspect with the broken nose), Meaachou Bentahar (Claude), Mohamed Ayari (Momo), Abdel Kader Touati (Maxime), Yann Dedet (Dédé)

Awards: Best male actor to Gérard Depardieu, 1995 Venice Film Festival

Sous le soleil de Satan (Under the Sun of Satan), 1987, 113 mins, col.

Production: Erato Films, Films A2, Flash Films, Action Films

Scenario: Sylvie Danton, adaptation: Maurice Pialat

Assistant directors: Didier Creste, Frédéric Auburtin

Photography: Willy Kurant

Editing: Yann Dedet assisted by Nathalie Letrosne-Wormserm

Continuity: Jacques Loiseleux

Sound: Louis Gimel

Settings: Katia Vischkof

Principal actors: Gérard Depardieu (Donissan), Sandrine Bonnaire (Mouchette), Maurice Pialat (Menou-Segrais), Alain Artur (Cadignan),

Yann Dedet (Gallet), Brigitte Legendre (Mouchette's mother), Jean-Claude Bourlat (Malorthy), Jean-Christophe Bouvet (the horsetrader), Philippe Pallut (the quarryman), Marcel Anselin (Monseigneur Gerbier), Yvette Lavoguez (Marthe)

Van Gogh, 1991, 158 mins, col.

Production: Erato Films, StudioCanal +, Films A2, Films du Livradois in conjunction with Investimages 2 and 3, Cofimage 2, the CNC and le Club des investisseurs

Assistant directors: Marie-Jeanne Pascal

Photography: Emmanuel Machuel, Gilles Henry

Editing: Yann Dedet, Nathalie Hubert, Assisted by Pierre Molin, Eric Renault

Sound: Jean-Pierre Duret

Sets: Philippe Pallut, Katia Vischkof

Principal actors: Jacques Dutronc (Van Gogh), Alexandra London (Marguerite Gachet), Gérard Séty (Gachet), Bernard Le Coq (Théo), Corinne Bourdon (Jo), Elsa Zylberstein (Cathy), Leslie Azzoulai (Adeline Ravoux), Jacques Vidal (Ravoux), Lise Lametrie (Mme Ravoux), Chantal Barbarit (Mme Chevalier), Claudine Ducret (the piano teacher), Maurice Coussoneau ('Chaponval'), Didier Barbier (village idiot), Gilbert Pignol (Gilbert), André Bernot (singer of the 'Butte rouge').

Le Garçu [from the Auvergne dialect for *The Son of* ...), 1995, 102 mins, col.

Production: PXP productions, France 2 Cinéma, DD Productions, Glem Films

Photography: Jean-Claude Larrieu, Gilles Henry, Myriam Touzé

Editing: Hervé de Luze

Sound: Jean-Pierre Duret

Sets: Olivier Radot

Principal actors: Gérard Depardieu (Gérard), Géraldine Pailhas (Sophie), Antoine Pialat (Antoine), Dominique Rocheteau (Jeannot), Fabienne Babe (Cathy), Elisabeth Depardieu (Micheline), Claude Davy (the *garçu*), Isabelle Costacurta (Isabelle)

Select bibliography

See also the References sections at the end of each chapter.

Books on Pialat

Fontanel, Rémi (2004) *Formes de l'insaisissable: le cinéma de Maurice Pialat*, Lyon, Aléas éditeur. A study of Pialat's films which came out too late to be considered or included in this book. Fontenel indicates he was inspired by work on Yazujiro Ozu and studies by Jacques Aumont.

Magny, Joël (1992), *Maurice Pialat*, Paris, Cahiers du cinéma. Until the publication of Fontanel's study, this was the only monograph in French available on Pialat. Elegantly written, penetrating and nuanced, it is a study of the themes and formal 'figures' of Pialat's work up to *Van Gogh*.

Mérigeau, Pascal (2002), *Pialat*, Paris, Editions Grasset & Fasquelle. The closest thing available to an official biography, providing invaluable biographical detail and devoting a chapter to each of Pialat's films, but disappointing in its unremitting emphasis on Pialat as a colourful character.

Maurice Pialat. L'enfant sauvage (1992) Museo Nazionale del Cinema. Catalogue published under the direction of Sergio Toffetti and Aldo Tassone in conjunction with a retrospective of Pialat's films at the Festival France Cinema in Florence. A beautifully done Franco-Italian edition containing many valuable articles (some reprints) by French critics, a revealing article on Pialat's reception in Italy, several important interviews, many stills and set photographs.

Book chapters and articles

Amiel, Vincent (2001), *Esthétique du montage*, Paris, Nathan. Devotes a lengthy chapter to Pialat as a key example of what he terms 'le montage de correspondances'. Amiel draws attention to a crucial formal feature of Pialat's mature work generally obscured by the attention given to his realism.

Forbes, Jill (1992), 'The Family in Question', *The Cinema in France: after the New Wave*, Bloomington, Indiana University Press. An important assessment of Pialat's work, the first in a book length study in English, identifying sexual relationships and the family as the focal points of his work.

Frodon, Jean-Michel (1995), *L'Age moderne du cinéma français*, Paris, Flammarion. Frodon's comprehensive history of film from 1950 to 1995 devotes important sections to Pialat as an *auteur*.

Powrie, Phil (1997), *French Cinema in the 1980s: Nostalgia and the Crisis of Masculinity*. Powrie's introduction provides important background to Pialat's work in the 1980s and the chapter 'A fistful of polars' provides a valuable perspective on *Police*.

Vincendeau, Ginette (1990), 'Therapeutic Realism: Maurice Pialat's *A nos amours*' in Vincendeau and Hayward (eds), *French Film: Texts and Contexts*, London/New York, Routledge. An excellent piece on what is arguably Pialat's greatest film.

Scenarios and analyses of individual films

Pialat, Maurice (1962) *L'amour existe* in *Avant-scène du cinéma*, no. 12.

Pialat, Maurice (1973) *Nous ne vieillirons pas ensemble* in *Avant-scène du cinéma*, no. 134.

Pialat, Maurice (1984), *A nos amours: scénario et dialogue du film*, Paris, L'Herminier. Not a shot-by-shot analysis of the film, but transcription of the dialogue with some indications about the *mise en scène*. It includes very valuable and revealing interviews with Pialat's actors and collaborators.

Pialat, Maurice (2003), *Van Gogh* in *Avant-scène du cinéma*, no. 534.

Philippon, Alain (1989) *A nos amours de Maurice Pialat*, Crisnée (Belgium), Editions Yellow Now. Two-thirds of this small book comprises stills from the film, some in colour, introduced by a short essay by Philippon and followed by reprints of interviews with Pialat's director of photography and his film editor.

Prédal, René (1999), '*A nos amours*': *étude critique*, Paris, Nathan. A volume in the Synopsis series. A thorough study that places the film in the larger context of Pialat's work, providing considerable background on the filming and a breakdown of the different sequences that focuses on sequence 19, the father's return.

Important interviews

Pialat, Maurice (1974), 'Trois Rencontres avec Maurice Pialat', *Positif*, no. 159.
Pialat, Maurice (1980), 'Entretien', *Cinématographe*, no. 57.
Pialat, Maurice (2000), 'Entretien: sur la colère', *Cahiers du cinéma*, no. 550.

Web site

www.maurice-pialat.net maintained by Rémi Fontanel, Professor of Film and Audiovisual Studies at L'Université Lumière Lyon 2, makes available bibliographical material, interviews, reprints of valuable articles and new research, as well as announcements of events or film showings that relate to Pialat's work.

Index

Note: page numbers in *italic* refer to pages with illustrations

QM LIBRARY
(MILE END)

WITHDRAWN
FROM STOCK
QMUL LIBRARY